Understanding Forescout CounterACT

Volume 1

Architecture, Configuration, and Troubleshooting

Marvin Greenlee

Understanding Forescout CounterACT, Volume 1

Architecture, Configuration and Troubleshooting

ISBN: 979-8-9861307-0-5

Warning and Disclaimer

This book is designed to provide information about Forescout CounterACT. Every effort has been made to make this book as complete and as accurate as possible, but no warranty or fitness is implied.

The information is provided on an 'as is' basis. The author and publisher have neither liability nor responsibility to any person or entity with respect to any loss or damages arising from the information contained in this book.

The opinions and views expressed in this work are solely those of the author and do not necessarily reflect the views of Forescout Technologies.

To Amarone, Desiree, and Julia

1. Table of Contents

About the Author

Marvin Greenlee has worked on hundreds of Forescout projects around the globe, including both professional services delivery and training. He was one of the first individuals certified by Forescout to deliver professional services and was certified as FSCE #3 in 2012.   Prior certifications include Cisco CCIE certifications in multiple tracks (Routing and Switching, Security, Service Provider), JNCIE certification from Juniper Networks, MCSE certification from Microsoft, as well as various certifications from CompTIA and other organizations.

Introduction

While Forescout is traditionally considered a NAC product Network Access Control or Network Admission Control, depending on initialism preference, the software provides much more functionality than just as an authentication platform.

The greatest benefit for many organizations is the visibility that Forescout provides, giving real-time information for who is connected on your network. Additional visibility through integrations allows the software to integrate data from a wide variety of other platforms. While the end goal may be restrictive control of who and what is allowed on your network, visibility is typically the starting point. You can't secure what you can't see.

The focus of this book is to provide a baseline for understanding general concepts of the product, getting started with the configuration, and providing awareness of some of the additional configuration items. Additionally, there are various troubleshooting items listed, both processes for troubleshooting, as well as specific commands for troubleshooting and information gathering.

Whether you are in the planning stages of your Forescout implementation or have been working with an existing implementation for years, there is most likely something to be learned. From pre-installation architecture questions that you should think through and be able to answer to various configuration settings to troubleshooting, this book covers a lot of information.

If you are just getting started, you may want to jump ahead to the chapter on Architecture, to make sure you are able to answer the high level questions about what you would like to do with the product.

If you are just getting started, the early chapters step through initial implementation with some tips and caveats along the way.

If you just bought the book because you liked the cover image that works too, and feel free to display the book on your bookshelf or coffee table.

I have tried to cover a variety of topics, so that people of all levels of experience with the Forescout platform can still find information that they haven't seen before.

In the interest of brevity, I have for the most part restrained from filling the book with screenshots, as that would easily more than double the size of the book, and the goal was to keep the book to a reasonable length. The general assumption is that if you are in the early evaluation stages, the questions in the architecture chapter don't really need screenshots, and if you have already started installing, then you will have your own Forescout environment to reference.

This book is not intended to be a replacement for engaging with Forescout support or to replace the usage of a certified Forescout Professional to deliver services or training for assistance with your deployment. Rather it is intended to serve as a reference resource.

Some of the items here are more complex. If you are new to the product, try to not feel overwhelmed if certain complex items aren't initially clear.

Any opinions expressed within this book are my own.

Don't try this at home. Or at work. Just kidding. For the most part, the commands and examples listed throughout are ones that I would consider "safe", however I have seen systems under load crash with even basic commands. Use caution and be aware that sometimes software does not always behave.

2. Device Initialization

In this chapter, we will step through the information needed for the initialization of the appliances and managers from the command line.

Command Line Initialization

Device initialization is started from the command line, and then additional initialization from the GUI.

If the environment only has a single appliance, then all configuration is done on that specific appliance. In most cases, you will have more than one appliance, and are likely to have an Enterprise Manager. The Forescout Installation Guide covers these steps in detail.

Single Appliance Steps:

Command Line Installation on appliance

GUI Initialization on appliance

Additional configuration on appliance

Multiple Appliance with EM Steps:

Command Line Initialization on EM

GUI Initialization on EM

23

Additional configuration on EM

Command Line initialization on each additional appliance

Add additional appliances to GUI on EM

Additional configuration per device

For the initial command line portion, you will need the following information for each individual device:

IP address

Subnet Mask

Gateway

DNS server

Hostname

Password

Is the device an appliance or an EM?

Is the device part of an HA pair?

Do you want to enable cert comply for enhanced security?

For an HA pair, each of the two devices in the pair will need it's own address, as well as an additional IP for the active device to use. For the first device in an HA pair, the first device is set up with all the information, and then when configuring the secondary node, you just need to tell the second node which is the primary sync interface and the password for the first node, assuming that you are using the default sync subnet.

For the most part the initial CLI wizard is straightforward. At the end of the process a summary is listed with the options of Test, Reconfigure, or Done. Review your settings as shown in the summary and select the test option (T). It will try to ping the gateway and try to resolve forescout.com via the DNS server that you have specified. If the gateway is configured to not respond to ping, that test may fail, but it doesn't mean there is any problem with the device being able to reach devices in the network. If the DNS server is only able to resolve internal DNS records, the test for forescout.com may fail, but DNS may still be able to resolve internal hosts without any issues. Afterwards select the option D for done, and it will save settings and restart services on the device with the new settings.

You will then be prompted to launch the GUI to continue.

3. GUI Installation and Wizard

In this chapter we will be covering the overview of installing the GUI and stepping through the initial wizard in the GUI.

GUI Install

The GUI can be installed for Windows, Linux, or Macintosh. For Windows you can download from the web portal of the appliance or EM with the address of the device (appliance or EM) in the browser, followed by /install. As an example http://10.10.10.10/install if your appliance or EM had an IP address of 10.10.10.10. For Linux or Macintosh, newer versions may not have the console available on the web portal, and if so, you will need to download from the Forescout website.

For the most part the installation is pretty straightforward. The only item to be cautious of typically is to make sure you are installing to a location where your user account has full access to be able to write files.

Launch the newly installed application and enter your IP address of EM or appliance. The user name for the GUI will be "admin" and the password will be the password entered during the command line setup. When logging into the GUI, you will be prompted to log in to the support portal. For now, select "Ask Me Later" at the bottom. Configuring additional login users will be covered in a later chapter.

GUI Wizard

For the GUI wizard portion, you will be progressing through the following steps:

- License - given the option to add a license here (can also be added later)
- Time - NTP settings for your environment
- Mail - mail relay information (if needed)
- User Directory - Service account information for the User Directory
- Domains - Service account information used by HPS
- Authentication servers (optional, will discuss more later)
- Internal Network
- Enforcement Mode
- Channels
- Switch
- Policy
- Inventory

For the most part these items are all straightforward. Many of the items can be skipped and you can configure the items later from the Options menu. If your session gets interrupted, you will need to restart the wizard from the beginning, so in most cases it's easiest to quickly configure and finish the wizard, even if that means coming back later via the Options menu to configure these items.

The Mail section defaults to box checked for mail relay. If you have a mail relay, enter the mail relay information. If not, uncheck the box. For email notifications the appliance will send emails to the mail relay (if configured), or directly to the destination SMTP server. If you DO have a mail relay, typically these will require adding the Forescout devices as valid senders, since a properly configured mail relay will not typically allow just anyone to relay.

The Domains entry is used to populate the HPS Inspection Engine, although that may not be evident from the listing in the initial GUI wizard. Authentication servers will be auto populated based on your entries entered for user directory, we will discuss this further in the chapter on the Options menu for what additional entries you may want to add here.

The Internal Network is used to define broad range(s) for your network address space. For example, if your internal network uses various subnets of the 10.0.0.0/8 address range, you could put the entire range of 10.0.0.0-10.255.255.255 as the internal network range. We will discuss this further in the segment manager design section later in the book. In newer versions it requires a segment name and it will require a range to be defined to proceed.

Enforcement mode allows you to select full enforcement or partial enforcement. In most cases there are no issues with selecting full enforcement, as it only affects traffic injecting traffic as channel response, and we don't have any of those actions currently enabled. We will discuss Enforcement mode in more detail later in the Options chapter.

If configuring an appliance, channels configuration will allow you to configure monitoring port information in order to enable appliances to receive traffic from the network switches or infrastructure.

For the switch item, you can skip for now, or just add one or two switches. We will discuss switch items later in the Options chapter.

The Policy item gives the option to auto create two policies for classifying devices and detecting guests. For now, it's usually recommended to uncheck these boxes if you are planning on a typical deployment using the Forescout Professional Services Policy set. Behind the scenes, these check boxes utilize the built in templates for Primary Classification and Guest. Policy Templates will be discussed later in the policy chapter.

The Inventory item configures basic information gathering policies for inventory policy. We will discuss these further in the Options chapter.

When you finish the wizard, it will save the configuration and restart the system services on the device (appliance or EM), loading the new configuration.

After the initial configuration, you can log in over the network via SSH using the username of 'cliadmin' and the password set during the initial command line wizard.

The cliadmin account has limited access. It allows some basic Linux command for checking connectivity, as well as some of the Forescout commands. The Forescout commands normally start with 'fstool', but when logged in as cliadmin, you can just type the commands without prefacing them with 'fstool'.

In order to see a list of the commands available, you can type '?' at the command line.

ping

This command can be used to test connectivity to other IP addresses

traceroute

If there is not connectivity, traceroute can potentially indicate where along the traffic path the problem is located.

linktest (or fstool linktest)

This command is the test that is run during the command line wizard to check link, gateway, and DNS.

tcpdump

Packet dump for traffic on the interfaces

reboot

reboot the device

user

The user command is available when logged in as cliadmin, and allows you to create new users. Users can be one of the following roles:

CLI Admin

Operator

Auditor

SecureFTP(only)

New users have a 9 character password requirement. Some passwords may give an error of "bad password" but they still may accept them. Users can be added, deleted, or have their permission levels changed.

Operator is similar to CLI Admin, but the operator role is unable to create new users.

Auditor has the ability to list files and view logs. Although tech-support is listed in the command listing, it does not have the ability to actually run the command, at least in the versions tested at the time of this writing.

SecureFTP allows SFTP access to the /shared/shared /shared/oslog and /shared/log folders. Access is read-only. If they will also need to upload to these folders, log in as cliadmin, connect via shell command to get root access, and then use chmod to adjust the folder permissions. Additionally, if the individual with the SecureFTP role needs to retrieve files generated by a tech-support, that tech-support would need to be saved to one of these directories, such as /shared, rather than the default of /tmp.

Sample of commands available for auditor:

auditor@myem>?

Available commands list:

!   - Execute command from history by id

?   - List of available commands

anonymize   - Anonymize files

clear   - Clear screen

exit   - Exit

help   - List of available commands

list   - List files/folders

monitor   - Monitor tail of the file

quit   - Exit

search   - Print line match a pattern

tech-support - Technical Support

view   - View files

auditor@myem>

auditor@myem>view

Use the view command to view log files saved by CounterACT in the 'log' folder, operating system logs saved in the 'oslog' folder, or shared files that were saved in the 'shared' folder.

Example:

  view log:watch_dog.log

  view log:plugin/va/va.log

  view oslog:audit/audit.log

auditor@myem>

Setting a shell password
The password that you set during the wizard is used BOTH for logging in by SSH with the cliadmin account and for the GUI with the account name of 'admin'. When logging in by SSH, the cliadmin account is limited to some basic commands. In previous versions you would log in directly as root. Due to security enhancements, this option is restricted in newer versions. In order to get to root access while logged in as cliadmin, first set a password with the command 'shell set-password', and then while logged in as cliadmin you can enter the command 'shell' and be granted access to the root shell. The shell password requires high complexity, and if you do not meet the requirements, it will let you know.

4. GUI Interface

In this chapter we will review the layout of the GUI interface.

Dropdown Menus

Across the top, we have a list of dropdown menus.

Just below that on the left we have the Forescout logo. On the middle we have a grouping of tabs

On the far right we have a gear that is an alternate mechanism to take you to the Options menu.

Panes

Below that, we have our four main panes.

On the left side at the top we have the Views pane, and at the bottom, the Filters Pan

On the right side, if you still have the map enabled you will see the map pane on top and the hosts and details panes below.

If you have disabled the map the Hosts pane will be on the top right, and the details for the selected host will be on the bottom right.

Drop Down Menus

File

The first entry 'File' has two options - log out and exit. While these may seem similar, log out will relaunch the console. In previous versions, the file menu also include a dangerous option for 'stop all policies', which fortunately has been removed, as it could cause issues.

Next over, 'Reports' has options for various reports. Policy report will give you a file of all the policies you have configured, threat protection will give you a report of items detected by the threat protection functionality. The top option "Reports" will take you to the reports portal.

Actions gives a variety of actions that you can apply to the selected host(s) in the host pane. Alternatively, you could just right click on a host and get the same listing of actions.

Tools

This menu gives various links to different configuration pages. Most common is selecting the "Options" entry to go to the options menu. Group Manager, Segment Manager, Ignored IP Manager, Threat Protection, and Appliance Management are shortcuts to jump directly to the configuration for those sections.

The assets portal selection here will open the legacy assets portal. We will briefly discuss both the legacy and new assets portals in the portals chapter. Additionally, this menu has an option to check for updates, and an selection available for

Change Password, which can be used if you are using a local account.

Log
The log menu allows you to directly display some log items. Policy log can show a history of policy information, either for a single host or for a range.

Host details can also be accessed just by double clicking on a host entry. Service Attack History will show a history of items detected by Threat Protection. Event Viewer will show login and logout activity and some system items. Audit trails will show actions and configuration changes made by administrators.

Display
Display has options for "more space" or "less space". This will affect the vertical spacing between lines in the interface.

Help
This menu provides links to the administration guide, the Forescout Website, Release Notes for the major version, and the Documentation Portal. About will show your system versions.

Note: The Administration Guide is local on the device, so you can still access it even if you are somewhere without internet access.

Home Tab Panes

Views, Filters, Detections, and Details

Views Pane

The panes vary slightly depending which tab you have selected. Views, Filters, Hosts and Details are the panes shown when you have the home tab selected.

Starting in the upper left, the Views pane lets you View all hosts, or just hosts that match a specific policy, policy subrules.

Additionally the Views pane also has a selection for Compliance and Corporate/Guest. In order for these items to be populated, you will have to have hosts categorized as compliance or Corporate/Guest category types.

Also of note at the bottom of the list in the views pane is the "History" option. So if you want to see how endpoints matched a specific policy last Wednesday at 2PM, you can see that, as long as the endpoints haven't been purged due to the inactivity timer.

Filters Pane

The Filters pane allows you to further refine the selection. For example, if you want to select hosts just from a specific segment or group, you can make that refinement here.

The Views and Filters pane have a search box at the top. For example, if you had a large list of segments and one was named NYC, you could just type NYC in the search box for the Filters and then select that specific segment, rather than needing to navigate through a long list of segments.

For the Views and Filters pane, typing something in the search box will restrict what you see in that pane, but just using the search box doesn't change your selection. For example, if you have group windows selected and then type NYC in your filter search box, it will show your NYC segment in the filter pane, but you still have group Windows selected.

The filters pane will let you select ONE filter. So you can't select BOTH 'segment NYC' AND 'group Windows' at the same time in this pane. You can make more complex selections like this in the new Assets portal, which will be discussed later.

Detections Pane

Only items that match BOTH the selected View and the selected Filter will be listed in the Detections pane on the upper right. One common error is to forget to remove a filter, and then wondering why you don't have the expected results in the Detections pane. For example, if you have the Windows subrule selected in the views, but your Filters pane has the printers group selected, you may not see any hosts listed in the detections pane. The top of the host pane gives an additional list of checkbox filters and dropdowns. The checkboxes available will vary based on what line you have selected in the views pane. All hosts, for example, will give a checkbox for "show only unassigned" and a dropdown to select online, offline, or both.

For policies, you will have options such as match, unmatch, pending, and irresolvable.

The search box at the top of the detections pane will act as an ADDITIONAL filter. So it can be very easy to accidentally restrict items that you see, as even a space would restrict further. You can search for various items, but the search result MUST be in one of the columns you have below. You can add and remove columns here, additional columns are available based on what plugins and modules you have installed. So, if you had the column for "NIC Vendor" as one of your displayed columns, you could type 'Apple' or 'Lenovo' in the search box at the top and only see hosts that matched that additional filter. Additionally, the detections pane search box can check for multiple items with commas between, or you can search by a partial IP or MAC address. Searches here are case insensitive.

'Apple,Lenovo'

This would match either Apple or Lenovo, since the two strings are separated by a comma.

10.99.1

This will look for a string-based match for the columns displayed with a value that includes this string. It could be the IP address of an endpoint, the value for the switch IP where an endpoint is connected. As an example, it would match all the following and many more:

10.99.1.1

10.99.10.34

210.99.1.35

14.10.99.1

Note: The new assets portal (also called assets view) allows searches even among columns not displayed, so it can be more robust in some cases for searches.

Advanced TIP: We mentioned that you can use commas if you want to match separate values. But what if the item that you want to search for actually contains a comma, like a DHCP request fingerprint. Well in that case you can use ? as a wildcard. So to search for '1,121,3,6,15,108,114,119,252', you could use '1?121?3?6?15?108?114?119?252' as your search string. Wildcards are not supported in all search boxes.

Host Exports

One other powerful option available from the detections pane is the ability to export hosts to a CSV. You can select one or more rows and then right click and select 'Export Table' at the top of the pop up menu. You can also select one row and then Ctrl-A to select all rows, and then the right click will export the entire host list matching the count in the upper right, which reflects the combinations of selected view and filters. Typically when exporting you may want to remove the columns that you are not interested in first.

For the export you have the option to export as PDF or csv. Typically csv is more common as it allows further manipulation later. We will take a look at an example of data manipulation later in the advanced chapters. Additionally you will be prompted for filename. You also have checkbox items for "exporting only selected devices' or 'only displayed columns'. Typically you will want both of these boxes selected.

Details Pane

The Details Pane will show the details for the selected host in the detections pane. Depending on which item you have selected in the Views pane, the Details will show either three or four tabs at the top. If the Views pane has a policy or subrule selected, the first tab will be the name of that policy or subrule, and the other three will be Profile, Compliance and All policies. The profile tab will show a list of endpoint properties resolved by discovery or policy. The Compliance tab will show whether the host is compliant or noncompliant for any categorized compliance policies, and the All Policies tab will show whether a host matches or doesn't match each and every policy configured. For policies that you have matched, you can see how the endpoint evaluates against those policy subrules. Additionally, to the right of the policy, there is also a button "View Policy Flow" to see what policies were matched that led to a policy matching a specific policy.

Asset Inventory Tab

This information is populated by the base discovery and inventory policies as well as the policies that you configure within policy. At a high level this tab allows you to do ad hoc searches of various properties. The difference with is that items are grouped by property, rather than by policy. The resulting detections pane shows the counts, and the lower right pane lists the individual hosts.

If properties are not currently in the inventory policy, you will be prompted asking if you want to add the policies. This prompt can get annoying, however, so it the prompt can be disabled under Options-Discovery by deselecting the checkbox at the bottom "Prompt user to add properties to the Inventory Discovery rule."

Sample checks

For example, you could select Windows Applications Installed and type Java in the top middle search box to see different Java versions and endpoint counts in the environment. Or you can select Users and sort by number of Hosts, to see where you have user accounts that have the same account logged into a large number of endpoints. Or you could select the property Windows Version to see if you still have Windows XP or Windows 7 in your environment. Other common checks here would be things like looking for specific ports open. How many devices do you have with telnet or ftp open? Do you have devices with web servers listening on port 80 that you didn't know about.

Policy Manager Tab

Our Third tab is the Policy Manager. Here is where policies are configured. On the left side are the policy folders, on the right side are the listed policies.

For the policy folders on the left, you can add a new folder with the + sign, or edit names, delete selected item, or import/export policies The arrow pointing up is for export, the arrow pointing down is for import. In general, best practice is to have structured policy folders. Typically they are grouped by policy family. If you import, you are importing into the folder you have selected. If not careful, you may import policies somewhere other than where you meant to, but they can be moved afterwards. On the right side, pay close attention to the filter box at the top as well as the checkbox for "show subfolder policies". If you have the top level item of "Policy" on the left selected, and the checkbox at the top middle for "show subfolder policies", then it will show all your policies. Just like the detections pane on the home tab, the search box at the top can drastically affect what results show in the list below.

One other thing to be aware of is that if you have a large number of policies, you will also have a scroll bar along the right side, just to the left of the Add button.

The buttons on the right side are for adding and editing individual policies, where the + on the far left is for adding a policy FOLDER, not a policy.

One of the most important things to remember with the policy manager is that no matter how beautiful your policy is, if you don't click apply when you are done, the policy can be gone in an instant. We will talk about policies more in later chapters.

Threats Tab

In older versions, threat protection showed up automatically and caused confusion for people that didn't understand it. In newer versions you have to explicitly enable to show the threats tab. If you don't see this tab, you can enable it under Options-Threat Protection - Show Threats View. We will talk about threats more in a later chapter.

Dashboards

The dashboards Tab launches the dashboard web portal, and you can also see a tab on the dashboard tab at the top to launch to the new assets portal. Unlike the Home and Inventory tabs, the new assets portal allows the option to select multiple filters concurrently.

*Technically the new assets portal is called "assets view" in some of the documentation. In many cases it is called an assets portal.

...

This three dot listing gives additional options to connect to assets portal (legacy), reports, and User Portal Builder. The User Portal Builder allows you to customize the look and feel of sponsor pages, as well as the HTTP notification and HTTP login pages. Common customizations are typically adding an organizations logo or using organization color scheme.

As mentioned earlier, the last item across the top at the far right is a gear which will take you to the Options menu.

5. Options Menu

In this chapter we will be reviewing the Options Menu, one of the main locations for configuration of the Forescout environment.

The Options menu is one of the most important sections of Forescout configuration. If items are misconfigured under the Options menu, then your Forescout database will not be properly populated with endpoint properties, and policy results may not be what you expect. Some of the configuration items here such as plugins and modules will have test buttons available or obvious identifiers like a green check mark. In many cases, items are misconfigured or underconfigured, often due to lack of understanding of what should be configured here. In this chapter, we will go over the major items in the Options menu as well as common misconfigurations.

From the main GUI screen, you can get to the Options menu by selecting the gear in circle in the upper right, or by selecting Options from the Tools menu at the top.

From a visibility perspective, the MOST important items under the Options menu are typically the following four items:

- Internal Network
- Switch
- Wireless
- Channels

We will discuss these in additional detail in this chapter, in addition to other key items in the Options menu.

At the very top on the left is a search box. You can type in a partial entry and items that match will show in the list under the search box.

Note:

For many sections of the Options menu, changes need to be applied before closing the Options menu or navigating to a different section of the Options menu. If you forget to select apply, a popup will show "Changes not applied, do you want to continue?". Be VERY careful with this box. If you click YES, any changes made are lost.

You MAY occasionally get the message "Changes not applied, do you want to continue?" even when no changes were made. If you get this when you have not made any changes, you can select "YES".

Additionally, some of the selections of the Options menu have a pencil and a '+' sign, indicating the ability of having multiple device groups.

CounterACT Devices / Appliance

If you are connecting to the GUI of an Enterprise Manager (EM), then the top line item will be "CounterACT Devices", whereas if you are connecting to an individual appliance, the top menu item will be "Appliance".

Here you can view the list of Enterprise Managers and Appliances and information about them including alerts, Description, and others. Selecting a specific entry will show additional information about that device or pair in the pane below. Additionally, you have the option to create folders and subfolders and place appliances into folders. For a larger environment this can be helpful for grouping appliances and maintaining structure, as certain configurations for various other portions of the Options menu (such as Mail and DNS) may have differing settings that you want to apply to a group of appliances, but not all appliances and folders can facilitate that.

At the top in the middle is a search box, and you can type in a partial name and match devices. In this field the question mark '?' can be used as a wildcard.

Just below the search box, as seen in other parts of the GUI you can add or remove columns. The available columns here are mostly appliance specific, common ones to add are things like CPU and Swap.

On the right side you have various buttons, most commonly used are the following:

Add - Used to add a new appliance (or HA appliance pair) to the EM

Upgrade - Used to upgrade the device to a higher major version (upgrade EM and then subsequently upgrade child appliances)

Backup - Used to take a manual one-time backup (scheduled backups are handled further down the Options menu, under Advanced - Backup, which will be discussed later in the chapter

Although there is a "Recovery" button here, that is not used to recover from a backup file, but rather is the mechanism by which a recovery manager is added. If necessary to recover from a backup, that is accomplished from the initial device configuration command line menu.

Additional sub menus under the CounterACT Devices line are IP Assignment and Failover and Failover Status. The IP assignment section is where you would assign IP ranges to the individual appliances, ideally the entirety of ranges covered by the internal network would be assigned out. We will talk more about assigning ranges in the Segment Design chapter. Failover clustering will be discussed conceptually later in the Architectural Overview chapter.

With regards to upgrades to the main system software, some organizations like to have the latest and greatest, where others prefer to wait until a new release has been available for a while, so that any initial bugs found will have had time to get fixed. In general, while I enjoy new features, in a larger environment I typically lean towards waiting at least a little while before upgrading. Additionally, if you have a development or test environment, it is strongly recommended to try new versions there on a separate instance before upgrading your main EM or EMs.

Channels

What is it?

The term "channel" in the context of the Forescout platform is a logical grouping of monitor and response interfaces.

Channels enable the appliances to ingest raw traffic feeds and take actions based on policy. Traffic would be captured, typically from a network distribution or core switch via a traffic replication method on the network side, such as a SPAN session, monitor port, VACL capture or other methods, depending on the particular switch hardware used in the environment. Traffic captured and forwarded can be tagged with 802.1q tags, in the event the sources had different VLANs used. Optionally, it can also receive a traffic feed from a third party device like a Gigamon or IXIA. The traffic feed is sent to a port on the Forescout appliance, and the Packet Engine ingests the traffic and adds relevant information to the database.

How to configure:

Configuring a channel requires configuring the monitor port, which is which port on the Forescout appliance receives the traffic feed, and configuring a response port. The response port can either be a dedicated physical port or by using the management port as the response port.

Configuring to use the management port as the response port is referred to as a "layer 3 channel" in some of the Forescout documentation. If a reply needs to be sent out, the packet is crafted and sent out the management port.

Configuring a dedicated port for response is referred to as a "layer 2 channel" in some of the Forescout documentation. In the event that the original traffic captured was on multiple VLANs, the dedicated response port can be configured on the switch side as an 802.1q trunk, and the Forescout platform will inject the traffic on the same VLAN where it was received.

While it is possible to have a Forescout implementation without any channels, it will limit some functionalities. Items such as the Threat Protection feature require configured channels in order to work.

Modules

Some of the modules have their own line entry in the Options menu list, where other ones are configured from the Modules entry.

A brief overview on Modules:

Originally they were called plugins, then some referred to as modules, then groups of them referred to as modules. In some of the documentation, the terms module and plugin are used interchangeably, but people that have been using the product for a while may still refer to them as plugins. There are three types: base, content, and extended. Base and content plugins/modules are ones that do not require any additional licensing. Many of these are included in the base system install, where others can be downloaded from the Forescout portal. Content Modules are additional information that is used by the modules. As an example, the HPS Inspection Engine uses the content modules Windows Applications and Windows Vulnerability DB. Extended modules typically require additional licensing. The Network module, as an example, includes the plugins for switch, VPN, Wireless, as well as a few others. In earlier versions, before these were bundled, plugins had to be individually upgraded. Now, rather than updating 30 individual plugins, the modules grouping plugins can be installed, installing a group of plugins at once.

Under the Tools menu, there is an option to "Check for Updates" which will check for newer General Availability (GA) versions of the modules that you have installed.

Optionally, you can connect to the Forescout Downloads page and download modules from there. At the time of this writing, the Downloads page is accessed by logging in at https://forescout.force.com/support and selecting the Downloads tab at the top. In order to log in to this page, you will first need to register with your organization's ActiveCare credentials and set up an individual account. Additionally, you may be able to get direct download links from your Forescout representative, in the event you need a version of a module not publicly available, or that is a hotfix or special build. In many cases, modules support rollback functionality, so if you have an issue with a specific new version that you deployed, you can roll back to the previous version. Typically the release notes will inform you whether a specific module does or does not support rollback. In general, it is always recommended to at least look over the release notes before installing a module or major release.

The top of the Modules page states "Modules extend CounterACT's capabilities by enabling integration with other tools". Sometime the information exchanged is only in one direction, bringing in properties about an endpoint, where other times there is also information sent out to the external item.

As an example, the switch plugin is two-way. We receive information from the switch via polling and/or traps, but also have the ability to SEND information to the switches in order to perform actions like applying ACLs, changing VLANs, and shutting down ports.

We will be reviewing the most common modules in greater detail throughout the next portion of this chapter.

One other key point to be aware of is that the help files for the modules are included with the plugin. So even if you are somewhere with limited or slow internet access, you have the help file right there on the box, and clicking the Help button for a module in the module list can download the PDF on your workstation from the appliance or EM

HPS Inspection Engine

This is one of the plugins that has it's own separate line entry in the Options menu. For the configuration of HPS, select the HPS Inspection Engine in the list on the Options menu. Some additional topics for HPS will be covered later in the Windows Manageability Chapter. For now, we will focus on exploring the base functionality. The HPS Inspection Engine is primarily used to manage Windows endpoints. Management is handled either via a service account that connects out over the network and has the ability to log into endpoints with administrative privileges, or by SecureConnector, which is the lightweight agent which can be installed on an endpoint in order to manage the endpoint that way. Some customers prefer agent based, some customers prefer agentless, and some prefer configuring both methods. If you entered credentials in the wizard, you should see them in the list here under remote inspection. If you have additional domains, you can add service accounts for other domains here as well. Forescout will try the various accounts and track what was used last for a host.

Before we get into the individual tabs for Remote Inspection, SecureConnector, and so on, notice we have a second row of tabs above remote inspection.

As mentioned earlier, when you see the pencil and the '+' sign, you have the ability to set multiple device groups. For example, you could have two different appliance groups, maybe you have different regions with different corresponding service accounts or differing domains used.

Remote Inspection Tab

When using agentless (service-account based), you have the option of selecting to use Remote Registry or WMI to query the endpoint. In earlier versions of Windows, such as Windows XP, the remote registry service was started by default. In newer versions, it is set to "manual" startup, and may not be running on your endpoints. An additional option here is "WMI with fallback", which will attempt to connect via WMI, and if that fails, will try via Remote Registry.

The script mechanism also has selections available. For WMI, you can choose between using WMI and using fsprocsvc. For Remote Registry, you can choose between fsprocsvc and using Task Scheduler. Task Scheduler is the older method which basically will schedule a task for a minute in the future. fsprocsvc is a small executable that gets pushed to the endpoint and is used to run scripts. By default, scripts are pushed to a folder in the TEMP directory of the endpoint. The HPS plugin help file details the ability to set an alternate script location if needed. The HPS help file also lists out specific permissions needed for the service account with regards to things like DCOM, logging in over the network, and so on, in the event your organization is security minded and likes to restrict service account privileges when possible. Additionally, the system can be integrated with systems like CyberArk where credentials are retrieved to be used, rather than stored locally.

Additionally on this first tab, there are options to specify an authentication method, either NTLMv1, NTLMv2, or Kerberos. NLTMv1 is not recommended due to security concerns. Additionally, there is the option to set a minimum SMB Protocol version. If you have older Windows endpoints that you are managing, setting this value too high will result in inability to establish a SMB connection. Requiring SMB signing is also a security restriction which will provide enhanced security, but will cause the Inspection to fail if the endpoint doesn't support it, or if certain devices are in the traffic path which are relaying SMB.

SecureConnector

The next tab for SecureConnector allows you to set various parameters for the SecureConnector agent.

In older versions, SecureConnector would automatically be upgraded to the newer version when there was an upgrade done to the HPS inspection engine. The first checkbox allows you to not automatically update. Some customers prefer to roll out the new version in a more structured fashion, rather than deploying all at once.

We will touch on actions a bit more later in the Policy chapters, but on this tab we also see some of the actions which require SecureConnector to be able to be run on the endpoint. Typically the boxes for "Automatically run" are left unchecked, and the box to show balloon messages is left checked.

SecureConnector ARP learning is the next checkbox. By default, when SecureConnector connects to the managing appliance it will report it's own MAC address. The option for learning the local ARP table allows for the forwarding of information about different hosts on the same broadcast segment as the SecureConnector client. One sample use case would be if you had a remote office where you didn't have switch manageability, but you did have SecureConnector on some hosts. By reporting the local ARP table of the endpoints that have SecureConnector, those endpoints can inform Forescout about other devices which are located at the remote office.

Password protection is another option, this will prevent someone from being able to just right click on the SecureConnector in the system tray and remove it, unless they know the password.

Additional appliance connections is not a common item, but there may be cases where you want to configure alternate entries to try to connect to different appliances, if endpoint cannot connect to it's managing appliance or to the Enterprise Manager.

Minimum TLS version can be specified here, but just like the SMB settings under HPS, if you have older clients that don't support a higher version, they will be unable to connect.

The HPS Inspection Engine also handles NMAP, so the tuning tab has an option to adjust the number of concurrent process threads. In general there is usually no reason to adjust these values.

And the last tab of "Test" requires entering an IP address if you want to use the Test button for the plugin. Without an IP address configured, the test button will not have a host to test. Additionally, not only do you have to enter the IP address in the test tab, you also have to click the Apply button to save the changes before using the Test button.

Guest Management

Since we haven't yet talked about policy, we will come back to this one later. At a high level, this section allows tuning of various Guest Registration items. At a high level, Guest Registration is triggered by an HTTP login action, with some of the parameters specified under the action, and the Options menu item for Guest Management able to specify some of the global settings here, such as who can sponsor a guest, password complexity, guest notifications, and other parameters.

User Directory

Often times the User Directory gets mixed up with the HPS Inspection Engine, partly because the same service account gets used for both typically, and partly because they may not have been properly explained to people. HPS is used for administratively connecting to Windows endpoints to check manageability using a service account. The user directory is used for the following purposes: Lookup user names in a LDAP directory like Active Directory to gather additional properties about the user, connect to authentication servers to authenticate users, either for web portal logins, 802.1x authentications, or logging into the console GUI.

Supported servers include Lotus Notes, OpenLDAP, RADIUS, TACACS, Oracle Directory Server, Novell eDirectory, or Microsoft Active Directory. Active Directory is most common.

To add a new server:

start with the Add button on the right side.

Set a name and select server type (default is Active Directory)

Select which functions it will be used for - user lookups, authentication, CounterACT login, Click Next

Enter IP address or (if an Active Directory server) select the checkbox for DNS Detection

Optionally, select a single appliance to use this new server (default is used by all)

For LDAP, port will default to 389, port 636 for LDAPS

Enter domain name and enter a user and password

If you have additional aliases you can add them below in the Additional Domain Aliases section.

Any will do a lookup against the domain, even if the domain doesn't match

Specify will allow you to specify a certain domain, or domains

Common use cases for Specify would be cases where the NETBIOS Domain doesn't match the domain FQDN. For example, if your fully qualified domain name was mycompany.com but your Netbios domain was MYCORP, then you could put MYCORP in the specify list.

When completed, click Next

The test tab has a spot for authentication server test user and a sample user to look up. In this case the user is populated from the previous page, however if you change the password in the future, you will need to make sure to change both locations when editing the User Directory entry.

After clicking Next, you are brought to the final setting for replicas.

Replicas provide an alternate mechanism of backup. The replica provides an additional server to use as backup.

For example, you can configure a server as replica, and the replica server will only be used if the primary cannot be reached. (Both are tested when utilizing the Test button, however)

Note: With regards to DNS detection, there is some misconception that it does a DNS lookup of the name specified for the server. That's not quite how it works. Rather it does a DNS lookup for SRV records to determine who is the Active Directory server for the domain. Additionally, DNS detection also relies on your DNS servers being correctly. One customer with appliances in multiple geographic regions had misconfigured DNS servers on appliances, and as a result, their User Directory implementation was using Active Directory servers that were several thousand miles away.

We will discuss configuring additional console users later and how to match to the server with "Use for CounterACT login" selected in it's User Directory server entry.

Switch

The switch plugin has a significant amount of functionality, both gathering properties and being able to perform restrictive actions. Proper switch plugin configuration will provide information about where all your wired endpoints are connected, and being able to restrict with methods including VLAN changes, applying ACLs, and even shutting down switch ports.

Adding a switch

On the right, start by clicking Add.

Start by configuring the address for the switch and the drop down for Vendor, click Next

Depending on the Vendor type, you may be prompted for either CLI or SNMP credentials (or both), click Next.

Set permissions - in most cases it is easiest to set both read and write actions. The first

For some vendors, such as Cisco, you will be given different options for read and write. For Cisco, you have the following options for MAC read/write:

Automatic - which method to use determined dynamically

SNMP (RW) - Uses SNMP for both read and write actions

SNMP (RW) and CLI - Uses SNMP for Read and write, CLI if needed

SNMP (RO) and CLI - Uses SNMP for Read and CLI for write

In most cases, you can leave it at the default of automatic, but some swear by using one of the specific other methods. Some customers only allow read access, for example, so SNMP (RO) and CLI would be most appropriate. For Cisco switches, VLAN changes and Port disabling can be executed via SNMP, but ACL writing requires CLI.

The button "Advanced ..." goes deeper into tuning settings and timers. In most cases, nothing needs to be adjusted under the advanced section, but the defaults are reading MAC tables every 60 seconds, polling ARP entries every 10 minutes, and doing switch discovery every 10 minutes. Typically the only one that most adjust is the discovery timer, as it is fairly unlikely that new switches would be added every 10 minutes.

When done with the permissions tab, click next at the bottom to move on to the ACL tab. If you plan on having Forescout use ACLs for control you will need to make sure to check the "enable ACL" checkbox.

Most customers aren't actively using SGT tags or wired 802.1x, so typically can just click the next button at the bottom and then the Finish button.

Now that the hard part of adding the first switch is complete, there are a few additional options available when adding a large number of additional switches, assuming the SNMP/CLI information is the same.

Two key features make configuring a large number of switches in the switch plugin much easier: discovery, and duplication. So can start by adding one switch and then duplicating/discovering others. If you do have a large number of switches in your environment, you will want to make sure that you balance them across appliances, so that a single appliance doesn't have it's resources overloaded managing a large number of switches.

Switch Discovery

Discovery allows you to discover neighbor switches via neighbor protocols CDP, FDP, and LLDP. Discovered switches need to be approved. For a large site, you can learn a large number of switches with just a few iterations of discovery. For example, in a traditional core-distribution-access campus, you could input the information for a core switch, run discovery and learn the distribution switches, approve those distribution switches, and then run discovery off of the distribution switches to learn all the access switches.

Switch Duplication

With one switch configured, if you know the management address for a few hundred or even thousands of switches, you can input the credentials to access one switch and then select the duplicate button on the right. You can then duplicate the settings to hundreds of switches by selecting the switch, clicking duplicate, clicking the option "duplicate to multiple IP/FQDN" and then the Import button on the right side of the Duplicate Switch window and reference a text file list of IP addresses, one on each line.

Now that we've added a switch, and discussed the options of discovery and duplication, lets talk about a few more pieces of the switch plugin. Along the top we have the now familiar layout of a list of columns and a search bar. Here the columns are specific to the switches. So we can add things like Switch hostname, OS, Query ARP status, number of MACs found, and other helpful switch relevant columns.

Switches can be bulk selected and edited. So, you could click on one switch and then use Ctrl-A to select all and then click the Edit button to edit them all at once (not recommended for large switch counts). Or you could use the search box to filter for just switches managed by a specific appliance, and select those.

The Test button for the switch plugin runs through a series of tests (typically 8-12) based on your particular switch plugin version. For items that you have not configured, the test status column will reflect "Not configured" or "Not applicable".

Right clicking also brings up a menu with most of the same selections available as the buttons on the right. Looking closely however, you may notice that right click menu brings up two separate options that both say Export. One at the top says Export Table, and the one further down just says Export. These are two different functions. Export Table, just exports the highlighted row(s) that you have selected in the table of switch columns. Export, however, is used to actually export the configuration for the switches highlighted in XML format. Additionally, since there are passwords, you will be prompted for a password to encrypt the potentially sensitive credentials.

Don't forget the Gateways

While it's called the switch plugin (or switch module), if you just configure your switches you may end up with an incomplete implementation. We mentioned earlier that we configured to read ARP tables, but the holders of the ARP tables MAY be switches, but they may not. In some cases they could be routers or firewalls or other third party devices. Looking through the Vendor list it may appear to be alphabetical, but if you scroll to the bottom you will see entries like Cisco ASA, Palo Alto Networks Firewall, and others. One of the MOST common errors I see when investigating an existing Forescout installation is forgetting to add the Layer3 devices that act as gateways for the respective networks.

One potential indicator that you are missing gateways would be if a certain location (or VLAN) is missing MAC addresses for many hosts.

Note: Because MAC addresses are learned from multiple sources, it is possible that you may be learning SOME of the

MAC addresses for a particular network, but others are missing. Windows devices, as an example, can reveal their MAC addresses via a NetBIOS query, where a printer on the same VLAN that is not running NetBIOS would not be seen with the MAC address property populated. Just because you are seeing a property, it may not be learned from the source that you expect. In the Details pane for a host, you can hover over the property value and see where it was learned from. In this case you would see that the MAC address for the Windows device was learned via NetBIOS, rather than via the switch plugin.

Additional settings for the switch plugin will be covered later in the Advanced Module Chapter

Wireless

Similar to the Switch plugin, but for wireless. The wireless plugin allows connecting to either AP or controllers

Depending on the vendor, some allow reading by either SNMP or Command Line, other ones don't have a selection option, based on how the plugin is written to interact with that controller/AP type. The wireless plugin has less configuration items and so is a little more straightforward. The default polling interval is 10 minutes (600 seconds) but can be adjusted if needed. RADIUS and 802.1x are outside of the scope of this section.

Mac OSX

Similar to the HPS plugin for Windows, the Mac OSX plugin is used to manage Macintosh devices. One key difference, however, is that the Mac and Linux plugins require you to explicitly enable remote inspection via a checkbox. When using remote inspection you will need to push the CounterACT SSH public key to the endpoints to manage, in order for the login to be successful. Be very careful with the "Generate new public key" as if you select that you are resetting the key and would need to push out the new key in order for hosts to accept the login. Just like with HPS, we also have the option of the SecureConnector. The Mac version is a complete app, so it is a bit larger size than the Linux and Windows SecureConnector.

Linux

Linux is very similar to the Mac OSX option. Checkbox to enable remote inspection, option of SecureConnector. There are several variants of Linux, however, and some that use different shells may not operate quite the same, so make sure to to some testing before wide scale rollout if you are planning to manage Linux endpoints using SSH.

Additional plugins and module topics will be covered later in the Advanced Plugin / Module chapter.

General

The general line entry expands to list the following configuration areas:

- Enforcement Mode

- SNMP Settings

- Mail and DNS

- Time

Enforcement Mode

Enforcement Mode allows you to select between Full Enforcement and Partial Enforcement. Some customers prefer to start with partial enforcement out of an abundance of caution. When in partial enforcement mode, the appliance will not send traffic out the channel response interface. The primary items affected are threat protection and HTTP actions such as HTTP redirect, HTTP Login, and HTTP Notification.

Notice the '+' next to the word Default. This means you can have separate tabs, and different settings for different groups of appliances.

Full Enforcement also has a checkbox option for NAT Detection. Multiple methods are used by Forescout to detect NAT. One method retransmits certain packets that are seen in the monitoring traffic. If the checkbox is not selected, this method will not be used.

SNMP Settings

Here you can configure SNMP settings for the Forescout devices themselves. This way, you can use a third party SNMP monitoring platform to monitor various MIB entries for the appliances themselves. Typical SNMP parameters can be set here, including restricting to specific views, configuring SNMP users, configuring Trap targets who will receive traps from the appliances, and Active Traps, to determine which traps you want the appliances to send.

Additionally on the General tab, you can Export the Forescout MIB. Technically, this file is not needed, since if you are looking at the button to export the ForeScout MIB you already have the file on your computer, as it is included in the GUI console installation. It can be found in the directory GuiManager\current\etc

Mail and DNS

Notice the Default Tab, you can have different values for different groups of appliances.

For mail settings, the default From: address when an appliance sends an email is Counteract@FQDN. If you want to use an alternate from: address, you can specify an alternate value here.

Operator email entered here will be used to send out system emails, and will also be the default when creating a 'send e-mail' policy action. Typically this is sent to a distribution group for the organization, rather than to an individual. When using emails as policy actions, you can specify an alternate recipient for that specific policy.

Mail relay may or may not be needed in your environment. One key point to test would be testing sending an email both to an email address internal to your environment, as well as sending one external to your environment, as sometimes you may need a mail relay for one of these directions. When using emails for things like Guest Registration, you may need the ability to send to both internal and external addresses.

The Default SMTP port is 25, if you select TLS the default is 587

The next item of Digital Signature allows you to digitally sign emails, assuming that you have imported a signed certificate in the certificate pane.

Time

The time settings allow you to set NTP server values. In the initial setup wizard you get an option to enter a single NTP server. In most cases you will want to use at least two NTP servers. Optionally you can set keys to authenticate the NTP responses. Previously, you had to set NTP from the command line, but newer versions have this available to set from the GUI.

Web Server Configuration

This entry allows you to enable HSTS, as well as the option to disable individual web portals.

Mobile Text Messages

In the event you are using Mobile Text Messages for things like Guest Registration, this allows you to enter settings to format for specific carriers. It can be sent as email or URL based. As an example, part of the Guest Registration can be configured to send a message to a phone number, in order to validate that a legitimate phone number was used for registration. If you have your own SMS gateway you can configure here to send to that gateway, or you can use various carrier formats for the prevalent carriers in your area.

Discovery

During the initial wizard you may have enabled the discovery and inventory policies. These gather basic properties about endpoints when the endpoints are learned by Forescout, independent of what you have configured in the Policy Manager section.

The default policy cannot be edited, your only option is to completely disable it by deselecting the checkbox. The Inventory policy can be edited to add additional properties, however it is recommended to be cautious before adding properties, for some properties it may be better to use a policy and only query devices where the property is relevant. For example, the property "External Devices" requires both that the endpoint is Windows AND that it can be managed, either by the service account configured in the HPS Inspection Engine, or by the Windows SecureConnector, so it makes more sense to just write a policy to query for this information, rather than trying to resolve the property on every endpoint in your environment. Additionally, you may have certain address ranges where you do NOT want to perform discovery. Leaving the setting of "All IPv4, All IPv6" would result in all endpoints within your defined Internal Network range having these properties evaluated. In some cases, a limited set of properties may be all that you are interested in, on just a limited group of segments. In that case, it may be preferred to uncheck these two, and create a new discovery policy for just the properties that you are interested in looking at.

We do have two checkbox items at the bottom, 'Resolve Properties displayed in the Console Information Panel' and 'Prompt user to add properties to the inventory Discovery rule'.

There are literally hundreds of properties available within Forescout. Just because you see a device in Forescout doesn't mean that those hundreds of properties are going to be resolved. Typically, properties are resolved based on what is configured here in the Discovery and Inventory policies, as well as properties gathered as a host is checked against the policies configured in Policy Manager. The 'Resolve Properties' checkbox means that if you add a column on the main GUI page, it will start resolving the property for hosts that match the filters and selections for your view. If the second checkbox is selected you will be prompted with "Would you like to add this property to the Inventory Discovery rule" EVERY time that you add a column on the main GUI page. As you may get tired of clicking "NO", it's usually easier to just uncheck the second box and not receive those prompts. It is possible, however, that if you add a column for a property that is not being evaluated, the column added will be empty and not have any results.

NAC
The NAC line under Options has the following entries

- Authentication
- HTTP Redirection
- Email
- Identity
- Time Settings
- HTTP Login Attempts
- Action Thresholds

Authentication
If you configured servers for User Directory during the initial GUI wizard, they will be added here automatically. Afterwards, if servers are added, you would need to add them here explicitly if additional servers were added later.

Servers and the relevant ports configured here are used in a couple other areas.

If the packet engine detects a traffic session to a defined server/port tuple, then it will match that and identify it as an admission event of "Login to an authentication server".

Additionally, if switchport ACLs are used, there is a checkbox option to "allow access to authentication servers", which would add entries to ACLs for the authentication servers specified here.

In large environments, it is typically not very practical to track all these servers and update here, and if using ACLs, the amount of overhead if there are a large number of lines here can cause resource issues on switch TCAM allocations. In my experience, most customers leave this section mostly blank.

HTTP Redirection

This section allows to add redirect exceptions, adjust for proxy ports, and also has links for the customization pages, both Legacy Customization and the newer, preferred User Portal Builder.

At a high level, HTTP Redirection is achieved by the packet engine parsing the HTTP traffic, and if there is a pending HTTP action for a host, to inject the HTTP redirect. When doing HTTP redirection, you typically are trying to redirect based on a user web session. There are times that there may be other items that use port 80, that are not actually user generated, and you may not want to redirect those. One example would be the URL "www.msftncsi/ncsi.txt" which is used by the Windows operating system to determine whether or not a network has internet access, and adjust the system tray network icon and show "internet access" when you hover on the network icon. Additionally, thinks like proxy pac files, or certificate revocation checks (crl) are items that you typically don't want to redirect, and they can be seen in the list of global exceptions. Another example would be that some antivirus vendors use port 80 to download virus definitions, so you wouldn't want to interfere with those.

If you have a web proxy in use in your organization, it is possible that the clients are configured to connect to an alternate port, such as 8080. If the packet engine is looking for traffic on port 80, and your endpoints are sending all their web requests on 8080, then the packet engine won't gather information correctly for your endpoint's HTTP flows. Another thing to be cautious of in environments where there is a proxy is where are you doing traffic capture and where is the proxy located. Some organizations do traffic capture out of what is leaving a site going out to the internet. If the traffic capture location that is being sent to Forescout is on the other side of the proxy, it will just look like web traffic is all coming from the proxy, rather than coming from the individual endpoint hosts.

The Legacy Customization tool is a bit limited, the User Portal Builder is more robust. In general, the point of customization is to change the look and feel of the Forescout pages. Common changes would be to match an organization's color scheme, and add things like organization logo.

Email

Email settings here are global settings, the default is maximum of one action per email. and a maximum of ten per day. There are a couple things to be aware of here. You have the option within a policy action to aggregate emails, but if you leave the default globally here of one, you will never actually aggregate and send fewer emails. Second, if you do exceed the total of these two values, an email will be send out that the threshold was exceeded, and then an email summarizing any other events will be sent out at midnight.

Trick Question: What time is midnight?

While it may seem like a basic question, in reality the point being made here is that midnight may not be when you think it is. This alert is based on when the appliance thinks it is midnight, which may (or may not) match up with other appliances. Even with NTP configured across your environment, it is possible for individual appliances to be configured for different timezones. Some organizations set all appliances to a fixed time, such as UTC or GMT, other organizations set different appliances to different time zones based on where they are physically located.

Identity

Normally, we consider a MAC address to be a unique identifier. What happens if the same MAC address is seen with a bunch of different IP addresses, or rapidly changes NetBIOS name? In this case, we have some internal settings here that basically decide that the MAC address may not be as unique as we thought.

So, running through the settings here. How many changes in what period of time and how long to ignore for. So with the default settings, if 20 changes are seen in a 5 minute period, that MAC address will be ignored for 1 hour.

The edit button will allow you see which identities have triggered, as well as be presented with an option to Add, remove, or edit entries. Typically most that you will see will be triggered by the switch plugin, due to the way some of the switch device internal MAC addresses are handled.

If you're seeing legitimate devices occasionally falling into this table, you may want to increase the count, so that more changes would have to be seen for it to be ignored.

One sample case where you may want to add a permanent exception would be for the situation of a remote access VPN termination point, such as a VPN concentrator. A VPN appliance may accept connections from hundreds or thousands of remote users, and hand out IP addresses from an address pool. In some cases, however, the VPN device has all the connected devices use the same MAC address, which corresponds to the MAC address of the internal interface. Since the same MAC address is used legitimately for multiple devices, adding an entry here to permanently ignore the MAC address will result in the Forescout appliance using the IP address to uniquely identify those hosts and they would not show up in the GUI with the associated MAC address. Without a permanent entry, you may see inconsistent results if there were just a small number of clients connected by VPN.

Time Settings

Here we have 6 global time settings.

Network Admission Resolve Delay

Policy Ignores Information Older Than

Inactivity Timeout

Purge Inactivity Timeout

Purge IPv6 Timeout

Display action icon after action complete

The first two can be overridden within policy with a 'per policy' setting available.

'Network Admission Resolve Delay'

This timer sets a slight delay time between when a host is first seen by Forescout and when active policy processing starts. The default is 30 seconds, and in some cases it is recommended to increase the value, where other cases (typically on a per policy basis) it may be beneficial to reduce the timer value.

The example given in the Administrator guide mentions services not running, so lets step through a little more of what that might look like.

Windows Endpoint receives an IP address

Services are still in the process of startup

Forescout scans endpoint as part of classification policy checking for Manageability

Unable to properly classify device since services haven't started and management connection fails

Device ends up as 'unmanaged'

At next policy recheck, device is properly classified as Windows Managed

In this example, having a slightly longer Network Admission Resolve Delay would ensure that the services had time to start, and the device would be properly matched as a Windows device in the policy evaluation.

Some examples when a device may take a while can include things such as full disk encryption or large group policy that may delay the service startup process.

What happens if the timer is too low?

Devices will not be properly matched, but will match the correct subrule after a recheck.

What happens if the timer is set to high?

Devices will be sitting on the network without being checked against policy.

At a high level the question you need to ask yourself is 'will asking sooner or later give me a different answer?'. If asking sooner will give the same answer, then it is OK to set to a lower value.

For example, if you have a policy that is just looking for a device with a specific MAC address, with a configured action to send an e-mail if it is seen on the network, then there is no need to wait 30 seconds or a minute. So for this policy, you could take advantage of the configuration option to set this specific policy for a lower value for 'Network Admission Resolve Delay' to a lower value like 1 second.

For reference, the location to change for a specific policy is to edit the main rule, select Edit at the bottom to the right of Advanced, and then on the General tab uncheck Default, and then set to the new desired value. Click OK to close the windows and save the changes.

'Policy Ignores Information Older Than'

Do you trust old information? Typically policies refresh based on the time based and admission based rechecks. This setting defaults to 3 days, the same as the default purge inactivity timer, but the two can be changed independently. In general, there is usually no need to change this value, I've personally only changed it a few times, due to some specific use cases.

'Inactivity Timeout'

This timer handles how long does a host remain idle before we presume it to be offline. The default is one hour. However, for the most part this only applies to hosts where we see channel traffic, but not where they are connected. If a host is connected to a switchport of a managed switch, for example, we will continue to consider it online as long as the switch is still reporting it's MAC address as connected on a port.

'Purge Inactivity Timeout'

After a device is offline, after what period of time do we purge it completely from the database. The default is three days, and I almost ALWAYS recommend that this value be changed. One typical concern is that items that have not been purged still technically count against the license totals, even if they are offline. Another point to consider is that if you purge too aggressively, you might lose forensic data.

One use case for a lower value would be a coffee shop or other location providing guest wifi. A coffee shop may have hundreds of customers in a day and they may not really care who was there 3 days ago, and might set a lower value of a few hours or a single day.

One use case for a longer value would be an organization that has vendors that visit once a week and use the guest registration provided wifi. Rather than having the vendor have to re-register each week, keeping their information in the system allows them to just log in again.

Many organizations will have an occasional long weekend, or holiday break. There's not much benefit in having to relearn all the same endpoints just because your purge timer was set to a value that was too low.

In general, I typically recommend a value of 2 weeks as a starting point, unless the organization has a need to keep longer. Additionally this is just a global value. You can also purge selected entries manually from the console or dynamically by policy.

One other note, this is only for inactive devices. If the device stays online, or even if it just comes online once or twice during the time period, the timer gets reset and the device properties will be kept indefinitely.

'Purge IPv6 Timeout'

IPv6 purge timing is significantly more aggressive, purging after 1 hour.

'Display action icon after action complete'

The final one is just a setting for how long to display the graphical icon after an item completes. Some recommend increasing this value to a week or two when you have newer administrators, but regardless of the setting, you can always double click on a host and look at the Policy Actions tab, to see what actions have been performed, either manually by an Operator or dynamically by policy. I generally just leave this setting alone.

HTTP Login Attempts

This setting allows you to set a threshold for the event HTTP login failure

Action Thresholds

Action Thresholds are a safety mechanism. For the more restrictive actions a low threshold is set. If the threshold is exceeded, the action is put on hold and will not be applied to new hosts that match. Action thresholds are across all policies on a per appliance basis.

As an example, the threshold for shutting down a switchport (switch block) is two percent. Say you have an appliance that has 1000 endpoints. If, based on various policy matches more than 20 hosts (2%), the switch block action will be put on hold. The assumption is that the thresholds are at a reasonable level, and that you would only exceed the value if there was a misconfiguration. You can adjust the thresholds if you expect to need a higher percentage in your environment. Additionally, you could exclude a specific policy from counting towards the threshold.

Once the action is placed on hold, it requires manual intervention to release the hold.

There may be cases where you expect a higher percentage. For example, if you have an appliance that is just doing guest registration, you would expect that appliance to have a large percentage of hosts with the HTTP login action.

Lists
Lists are used within policies. We will discuss lists in greater detail later in the Advanced Policy chapter. For now, just know that you can go to the lists section under Options to view or search list entries, or add, edit, or remove a list.

Map

The Map allows you to graphically show sites in your network. Segments are assigned to Locations, which can be configured by latitude and longitude or by street address. You can choose what is considered small medium or large sites, as well as compliance thresholds. There is also the option here to disable the map view, but if it is disabled here, it is disabled for everyone. Optionally, individuals can just resize the map pane out of the way in the main console GUI window.

Internal Network

The internal network is generally analagous to a perimeter fence. What is the entirety of the address space in use in your environment. So, if your internal addressing used is various parts of the 10.0.0.0/8 address space, you could set that range as your internal network. We will talk about the internal network more in the Segment Manager Design chapter.

Threat Protection

Threat protection is a built in functionality that monitors for possible malicious activity in the traffic seen by the packet engine. In full enforcement mode, it can react to the malicious activity seen, which can help block or restrict certain attacks. Threat protection will be covered more in the Threat Protection chapter later.

Access

This section allows you to restrict access to the Forescout device, either Console GUI or the web portals. The default is to allow from all IPs. At a minimum, typically the Console GUI would be restricted to internal addresses. If you have restricted networks, such as Guest networks, you may want to restrict those address ranges to just the HTTP Actions.

Similar restrictions can be made to restrict source address for the command line SSH access, using the command 'fstool ssh'.

CounterACT User Profiles

Here is where additional users are configured. You can configure local accounts, or reference an external user or group. For a local user, they will be subject to the password complexity specified in the Password and Sessions section which is the next line down. If you reference an external user or group (such as an Active Directory user), then that external source will handle the requirements for password complexity, rotation, and reuse.

In most cases, the recommended method is to use external group. External group is recommended because if a new person is added in the organization that needs access, you can just add them to the appropriate group, rather than having to create a new user. For example, maybe you give your network operations center (NOC) read access to the Forescout environment to investigate items. Rather than a bunch of individual users, you could reference your NOC group in Active Directory. In order to reference a group, you would select Group-External User Directory in the drop down for user type under the Add User Profile. You will then be presented with the Server Name to Next, select the permissions for the group. The View column is read access, and the Update column is change access. If you check the Update box for a row, it will automatically select the View box for that row as well.

Click Next to proceed on to Scope configuration.

Scope allows you to restrict hosts that a profile can view in the GUI. (Or write policy for those hosts, if you have assigned Update permissions as well.)

In general, security best practice is to follow the rules of least privilege and have different roles that only have the permissions that the individual roles need. For example, if your help desk staff just needs View access, then don't assign them Update permissions for anything.

One key additional point is to watch very carefully who you give update permissions for the row "User Management", as someone with those permissions could adjust their own permissions, potentially elevating their privileges with additional access.

Password and Sessions

Here, password complexity can be set, as well as various settings such as password reuse, locking after a certain idle time or failed logins, most of which are self explanatory. On the login tab you can specify login banners to show before or after login. Earlier when we first logged in for the initial setup wizard, we were prompted for customer verification. If you don't want to receive that pop up, you can uncheck the box on the login tab for "request customer verification'. The session tab allows you to configure whether you allow multiple sessions for the same user, and if you don't do you reject the new session or terminate the existing session, as well as session timeouts and idle timeout, as well as whether to try to reconnect if the session is dropped.

Smart Card
If using a smart card, this section lets you import the CA root and intermediate certs in order to validate the certificates on the smart cards.

External Identity Provider
This section allows you to configure an External Provider for the Forescout web portals, such as OKTA or PingID, or other SAML 2.0 compliant providers.

Console Preferences
Here is where you configure settings for your local console GUI installation, including the maximum memory for the Java virtual machine to use, time zone, HTTP proxy, where to save Threat protection reports locally, and setting alerts by severity level for Threat protection. If you have a large amount of memory on your endpoint where you have the GUI installed, it is recommended to increase the maximum memory. In earlier versions you were limited to 1500Mb (1.5Gb). In new versions, you can specify higher values, up to your devices total memory.

Advanced

Data Sharing
This line lets you opt in to Data Sharing with the Forescout Research Program

Overlapping IPs

In most cases, the IP address space is unique. If you have legitimate reasons to have overlapping address space, select the checkbox here first and then configure IP Reuse Domains.

In the past, overlapping IP space was not allowed.

Under the new configuration, Reuse Domains allow you to identify separate overlapping address spaces. For example, you might have branch offices that use the same IP addressing. When configuring other items such as the switch plugin, you would configure the switches at branch 1 with a different reuse domain than the switches at branch 2.

Backup

As mentioned earlier, you can perform a one time backup under the Counteract Devices section. The backup section under Advanced - Backup allows you to configure scheduled backups. You have the option to choose a protocol - FTP, SFTP, or SCP, set the location of the target server to save backups to, the directory and login information for the server. On the next tab over of Encryption Password, you get the opportunity to set a password for encryption, as you will want them to be kept secure, due to the sensitive information in the configurations. The next two tabs System Backup and Component backup let you set how many files to store, how frequently to occur and the time and types. System backup is a full backup, component backup just backs up specific sections of the configuration.

Component backup covers the following: Switch plugin, wireless plugin, policies. With the component backup it is not necessary to reinstall the platform. The full backup, either a scheduled system backup or a one-time backup taken from the CounterACT devices page is restored from the initial base software install menu.

Optionally, in some cases you can restore to a VM and then extract specific files if needed.

If the backup server is unavailable, then backup files will be stored on the EM. This can cause problems if your EM has an issue and the files are lost.

Additionally, other sections can be backed up individually. Segments, Groups, Policy, as well as switch and wireless entries can all be exported.

Performance Thresholds

Here we have threshold values for various alerts for CPU, memory, number of hosts, Channel Bandwidth, and packet loss. Typically there is no reason to adjust these settings.

Classification

The Device Profile Library just has a checkbox item available for configuration. If checked, the DPL updates are automatically applied when they are installed. In most cases, you will want to have this box UNCHECKED.

The Device profile library is used by the Device Classification Engine for determining device Functions, Operating Systems, and Vendor and Model Classifications.

New versions of the profile library may classify devices very differently. In general, the primary reason to NOT auto apply the DPL updates is so that you can review the changes and see what the differences are. The 'Pending Updates' section allows you to see the 'before and after' before applying the updates. In general, the updates are available for comparison after the endpoints go through a recheck, so typically most of the changes to Function, Operating Systems, and Vendor and Model can be viewed under 'Pending Updates' within 8 hours after the new DPL has been installed, due to common policy timing. Depending on the diversity of device types in your environment, it is possible that there are little to no changes when installing a new DPL version. Typically, the more specialty devices you have in your network, the more likely you are to see changes. If your environment is just Windows machines, printers, and IP phones, there may not be any changes after a DPL update.

6. Policy Overview

In this chapter we are going to go over the basic concepts of policies. More advanced policy concepts will be covered in later chapters.

Let's start with the minimalist overview.

Name, Scope, Main Rule

Name

Each policy requires a unique name. Generally it is recommended to keep your policy names descriptive.

Note: In the Forescout Professional Services Policy set, policies are given numeric identifiers as part of their name. For example, a policy name of '1.1 Primary Classification'. The reason for adding a numeric identifier at the beginning of the name is so that it is easy to find in a list, and the numbering format corresponds to the policy grouping.

Scope

Each policy requires a scope. For a generalized definition, the scope is the address ranges of endpoints that your policy will check. We will talk about more complex scopes in the Advanced Policy chapter.

Main Rule

Each policy requires a main rule. The main rule allows you to further refine based on specific conditions.

In general, we want Scope and Main Rule to be as granular as possible to minimize resources used for policy processing.

Now that we've covered the minimalist perspective, lets get a little more detailed and add some additional terms and details.

Scope and main rule is the starting point. Typically we will want to break things down further. This is done by adding sub rules to match various additional conditions.

A slight distinction between the terms properties and conditions. The property is the specific trait, and the condition is the value that you are looking for being present or not. For example, 'Operating System' would be a property, but 'Operating System is Windows' would be a condition.

For scope, you can select 'All IP addresses' which will include any endpoints in the defined Internal Network, or you can select one or more Segments where you want to apply the policy. Some policies, such as the initial Discovery policy configured using the Primary Classificaiton template typically are configured to be run against ALL hosts. Later policies may have a certain subset of hosts with the policy applied. For example, perhaps there is a policy that just applies to a single site or just one of several regions.

The primary classification template starts with a main rule condition of "No conditions". If the main rule is set to "no conditions", then it will apply to all the devices in the defined scope.

After matching both Scope and main rule, the policy then continues to process the policy, evaluating the endpoints against the subrules in order. If a subrule is matched, processing stops. If it doesn't match, it proceeds to check against the next subrule.

Typically the last subrule is set to "no conditions" which will act as a catch-all for endpoints not matched by one of the higher sub rules in the list.

Note: For a main rule or sub rule, 'No Conditions' is treated as a match all. For the Scope, if no scope is set, it is treated as 'match none', and no hosts will match the policy.

Creating a Policy

Policies can be created in a few different ways

1. Create from scratch

2. Create from template

3. Import a policy that someone else has created.

Primary Classification Template Policy
Initially it is usually easiest to start by creating a policy from a template.

In case you don't have the policy to reference, we will step through the process of creating the Primary Classification template policy.

Start on the Policy manager page by selecting the Policy button at the top of the main GUI screen.

- On the Right side select Add.

- Expand Classification and select Primary Classification, click Next
- Optionally change the policy name, click Next
- Select an IP range, for now can select 'All IPs', click OK, then click Next
- Click Finish
- Now click 'Apply' in the lower right to apply your policy changes.

Now that our template policy has been created, let's take a look at the high level overview of the policy components for this policy:

Scope - All IPs (Net result is to match everything in the Internal Network)

Main Rule - No conditions (Net result is match all)

The net result of the combination of scope and main rule is that all addresses in the Internal Network will match the policy and be evaluated

Subrule Windows

Is your Operating System Windows? If yes, match subrule and stop subrule processing

Subrule VoIP

Are you a VoIP device? If yes, match this subrule and stop subrule processing

Subrule Network

Are you a Network Device? If yes, match this subrule and stop subrule processing

Subrule Printers

Are you a Printer? If yes, match this subrule and stop subrule processing and so on for the remaining subrules.

Note: While devices are still being processed, you may see a device count showing as 'Pending' if you hover on a subrule.

Now if we just wanted a sorting of major device types, there would be nothing further to do. However, we want more than just a breakdown of major device types. The next part of the policy which we haven't yet discussed yet is actions. Actions are assigned to either main rules or sub rules. For our initial policy, we will be using the action of 'add to group', which adds endpoints to a logical group within the Forescout database. Later on in subsequent policies, we can use these groups to evaluate policies against smaller and smaller groups of devices, so that we are only evaluating against relevant devices.

Initially with the first few policies we are just sorting devices. Sometimes this is called a breakout policy, as you are breaking devices out into smaller groups to be referenced later.

Keep policies simple   It is better to have a few small simple policies than to try and group a large number of conditions together with overly complex Boolean conditions.

If you selected the checkbox for classification during the wizard or if you are working in an existing environment, you will already have an initial Discovery policy.

Editing a Policy

To edit a policy, go to the policy manager and select your policy from the list. Click edit on the right side or you can right click and select Edit. If you have the main rule selected, you can edit the entire policy. However, if you have selected a subrule, you will only be able to edit that specific subrule.

There are literally hundreds of different policy conditions available, and more are added with additional plugins and modules installed. Some of these conditions have additional prerequisites. Properties such as processes or installed applications require the endpoint to be manageable in order to check these items. Additionally, some of the actions will require specific prerequisites.

Initial visibility from the basic policy created by the Primary Classification template is predominantly driven by the properties of Function, Operating System, and Vendor and Model.

Basics of Policy Timing

By default, a policy will be checked when a device is first discovered, due to the device matching what is called an admission event. After that initial check, the policy will be rechecked periodically based on seeing additional admission events or by periodic timer. Some of the sample admission events include things like DHCP Request, Offline host became online, IP Address Change, Wireless host connected. The default timer for a policy recheck is 8 hours. So if another DHCP Request was seen 4 hours later, then the policy would be rechecked at that time. Otherwise the policy would be rechecked after 8 hours, based on the recheck timer. There may be cases where you want a specific policy (or subrule) to have a different timer, or only recheck based on specific admission events. A list of the admission events can be viewed under the Advanced button on the Main Rule of a policy.

Policy Conditions

For the initial policy created by the Primary Classification Template, the criteria used for subrules are mainly 'Vendor and Model', 'Operating System' and 'Function' which are primarily derived from the Device Classification Engine with inputs from the DHCP classifier and Packet Engine assisting to make the determinations.

Policy Actions

Initially, our policy here is just sorting devices, so our only action is 'add to group' which we will use later to scope later policies to a smaller subset than 'All devices'.

We will discuss policies further in the Policy Set chapter and the Advanced Policy chapter.

7. Introduction to Troubleshooting

In this chapter we will be taking an introductory look at the troubleshooting process. More detailed examples will be covered later in the advanced troubleshooting chapter.

There comes a time in virtually every deployment that something doesn't quite go as expected. Maybe it's a random error message, maybe a button doesn't work when you click on it, maybe your policy doesn't quite seem to be working the way you expect. For the purposes of this chapter, we are going to assume that you have a valid Forescout support ActiveCare coverage, and that you will be working through things with assistance from Forescout support.

Troubleshooting Steps
The overly simplified process is as follows:

1. Notice a problem

2. Gather basic information

3. Open a ticket with Forescout

4. Gather additional information as needed

5. Test suggested resolution(s)/workarounds

6. Success, problem is gone.

We are going to assume that you are referencing this chapter because you have already completed step 1 above. Lets start with some information gathering.

Step 2 - initial information gathering

If the problem is something that is visible in the GUI, take screenshots.

Next, connect to the command line via SSH and gather the output of the following commands in preparation for the next step.

If the issue is on the EM, you will want to connect to the EM. If the issue is on an appliance, connect to the affected appliance when gathering this information.

fstool sysinfo

fstool check_license

Don't close your command line (SSH) window, we will be gathering some additional information in step 4.

You can gather the serial number from the output of 'fstool sysinfo', optionally you can run the command 'fstool serial' separately.

Step 3 – Opening a ticket

Opening a ticket

The two most common methods for opening a ticket are opening online, or by phone. In the past, emailing support directly was an available option, but that option has since been removed. To open online, log into the support portal at https://forescout.force.com/support and enter your individual credentials here. You can also open by phone. Opening by phone is typically reserved for high severity issues, which are causing significant outage/impact in the environment.

Click on the Cases button, and "Contact Customer Care".

You will be prompted for the following information, which you should have gathered in the previous step. Be as detailed as you can with your description, including what observations you have made.

- Subject
- Description
- Severity
- Product
- Product Version
- Category

- Sub-Category

- Serial Number

- fstool sysinfo

- fstool check_license

If you have entered all the required information for the ticket, you should receive a ticket number. You will also receive an email reply. If you don't get validation that the ticket has been created, double check the page to see if you have any errors showing.

In addition to opening a ticket, while you're logged into the customer portal, it's recommended to search the Knowledge base, using the search box at the top of the page.

Additionally, you may want to post a synopsis of your issue to the community, using the forums button on the customer portal page. While not a replacement for support, the community can be another source of information that can potentially assist in resolving the issue.

Step 4 - Gather additional information

Now that you have the ticket number, you can reply to the email that you received, or you can add notes to the ticket online via the support portal where you are logged in.

Depending on your service contract, the severity of the case, and the time of day, their are different expected response times. For example, a high severity ticket during business hours will receive a faster response than a low severity case opened after hours with an ActiveCare Base contract.

FSTOOL Tech-Support

One common next step is to collect tech-support information.

The command 'fstool tech-support' will gather basic information which can be helpful to assist support with some additional information. Running the command with no additional options will gather general information for the previous 24 hours. There will be some prompts along the way, asking for things like Company name and comment, typically it is easiest to reference your ticket number in the comment. Sending directly to Forescout requires the appliance or EM where you are running the command to have access out to the internet.

We will go over some more complex examples later in the advanced troubleshooting chapter, but for now we will start with some of the possibilities and cover some basic examples.

Some of the types of things you can do with the tech-support command:

- Set a time range
- Select one or more plugins to include information
- Attach a file
- Attach a database table
- Review the file locally and not automatically send to Forescout

Setting a time range

As mentioned earlier, the default is to gather for the last 24 hours. If one time value is specified, the tech-support information gathered will be from that time period ago to now. If two time periods are specified, it will be from the earliest of the two to the later of the two (order doesn't matter). h for hours, d for days, m for minutes. Additionally, you can also use time formats such as linux epoch time. Linux epoch time can be easy to match time around a specific log entry timestamp.

Time examples

From 3 days ago to 2 days ago

fstool tech-support -t 3d -t 2d

From 36 to 48 hours ago

fstool tech-support -t 48h -t 36h

From linux epoch time 1650000000 to 1650001000

fstool tech-support -t 1650000000 -t 1650001000

from 4 hours ago to 10 minutes ago

fstool tech-support -t 4h -t 10m

When you run the command, it will display the start and end times

Plugin examples
Include HPS Inspection Engine and Switch Modules

fstool tech-support -p va -p sw

Version information and short plugin names

fstool tech-support version

Typically uploading a tech-support will give the support engineer a bit more information to try and identify the problem. Typically, if adding a tech-support to a case, it is recommended to add to the case notes or reply to the case email to let them know that you have uploaded a tech-support.

After reviewing the case description and uploaded information, the support engineer will either reach out with a suggested fix or possibly will ask to gather additional information. Depending on what the topic is, it may be scheduling a webex to observe the behavior you are experiencing, instructing you to gather additional log information or turn on some debugging or trace information, or upload additional files. Ideally, it will be a known issue with an easy to implement fix. If it is something that does not have a direct fix, they may inform you of one or more potential workarounds.

Overview of logging:

Logs for the appliance are mostly stored in the /usr/local/forescout/log directory and it's subdirectories. For several of the plugins/modules they each have a plugin specific directory under the /usr/local/forescout/log/plugins with the most recent being the short name of the plugin followed by the extension .log as the end of the filename. Older log files for the same plugin will have the linux epoch time as part of the filename.

For example, switch logs are under /usr/local/forescout/log/plugin/sw and the most recent is sw.log. In most cases, the logs are automatically attached if you use the relevant -p flags on the tech support command, so it is generally not necessary to manually download the log files.

Note: If you do need to copy files from an appliance or EM, Windows 10 and later supports scp from the command line, so you can copy directly from a command shell window.

Understanding epoch time

As mentioned earlier, some of the log files give date stamps with a time and date and other ones give epoch time. If you want to convert from epoch time to a more familiar format, you can use the commands 'fstool localtime' or 'date -d @' followed by the epoch time.

fstool localtime 16491234567

date -d @16491234567

If you want to see what the current epoch time is, you can use the following:

date +%s

Additionally, some of the references for endpoints use a numeric identifier rather than the dotted decimal format for an IP address.

If you want to convert between dotted decimal and the numeric format, you can use the following commands.

fstool ip2int 10.10.10.10

fstool int2ip 168430090

From a troubleshooting perspective, ideally you will be able to answer the following questions:

Does the issue affect multiple appliances?

If so, all appliances or just some of them?

What plugins appear to be affected: Switch, HPS, Wireless?

Do plugin tests run OK for the affected appliances?

Is it an issue with a device not matching a policy?

Does the device match the scope and main rule?

Is it an issue with devices matching a policy but not the expected sub rule?

Are properties not resolved? Is property information stale (outside the 'ignore information' timer?

Is it missing information that is not properly resolved?

Is it an issue with an action not applying after it has matched a specific main rule or sub rule with an action?

Is the action not happening at all? Or is it just delayed?

Does the appliance behaviour seem OK in other areas?

Does 'top' show excessive CPU or memory usage?

Sample issues

Switch Issues

Switch port information not resolved

- Verify switches and layer 3 gateways configured under switch plugin
- Verify switch plugin tests are successful for relevant switches and the layer 3 gateway
- Verify switch shows device as online

Switch change VLAN action not applying

- Verify port information resolved
- Verify VLAN exists on switch
- Check switch read/write method under permissions

For switch issues, it is recommended to increase debug level for the switch plugin and forward logs to support. 'fstool sw debug 5' is usually sufficient. If a different debug level is necessary, the support engineer will typically let you know what level to set the debug. Afterwards, turn off with 'fstool sw debug 0' or 'fstool sw debug stop'.

When increasing debugs for the switch plugin, make sure you are increasing the debug on the correct appliance, which would be the appliance managing the switch(es) in question.

117

Depending on how your environment is configured, this MAY be a different appliance than the one that is assigned to manage the endpoint.

In previous versions when you turned on a debug it was on until turned off, and potentially could end up filling up the disk on the appliance with log information if left on for too long. In newer versions, the plugin debug will turn off after 7 days, however it is typically best practice to limit even further, by setting a time range so that it will turn off in a reasonable time.

Examples:

fstool sw debug 5 1h

fstool sw debug 5 10m

If you are running multiple debugs you can also run 'fstool debug -l' to display the debug levels, so that you can confirm that you have disabled them all when you are done.

HTTP issues
Login / redirect action not applying

- Verify if device is shown as matching policy
- Verify policy tab shows HTTP action applied
- Verify if traffic seen on channel monitor interface (via tcpdump)
- Verify if traffic redirect sent out response interface (via tcpdump)

- Verify if endpoint receives redirect back, if possible (via tcpdump)
- Verify if endpoint can connect to web portal on the managing appliance (http://x.x.x.x/status , where x.x.x.x is the appliance IP)
- If using DNS enforce instead of traffic based redirect, use nslookup on endpoint to test DNS resolution

EM not connecting to a specific appliance

- Verify that you can ping the appliance from the EM
- Verify that you can SSH to appliance from the EM
- If appliance connection is by name, verify that EM is able to resolve the name of the appliance to an IP
- Check the output of 'fstool service status' on the appliance to ensure the services are running
- tcpdump on the appliance to see if it sees the TCP connection coming from the EM
- tcpdump on the appliance to see if the appliance is sending return traffic to the EM
- tcpdump on the EM to see if traffic is being received

Services not starting on an individual appliance or EM.

- Use 'fstool service status 10' or 'watch fstool service status' to see if the services startup is stuck in a loop.
- Review the trace logs at /usr/local/forescout/log/

- If looping service startup crashing, use 'fstool trace -t' to watch the logs as the services start and see if there is a specific error before the services crash.

Note: If you do find something of note in the trace logs, make sure to upload those log files to your support case.

Additional sample troubleshooting steps will be covered in the Advanced Troubleshooting chapter.

Introduction to Troubleshooting

8. Forescout Professional Services Policy Set

In this chapter we will be giving a brief overview of the Forescout Professional Services Policy Set.

In most cases, Forescout hardware is sold in conjunction with professional services to implement the product. If you inherited a pre-existing installation, you may have the policies there in place but not quite understand the structure of them. In this chapter we will cover a high level overview of the structure, as well as general discussion of some of the additional policies commonly implemented.

The point of the professional services policy set is to provide a structured starting point, which can then be adapted to the individual customer environment.

In the early days, the best practices policy set was called "the 4Cs", and consisted of the following four phases:

- Classification
- Clarification
- Compliance
- Control

In the newer policy set, the four primary policy families have been renamed to the following:

- Discover
- Classify
- Assess
- Control

Additionally, the newer policy set references the architectural breakdown of See, Control, Orchestrate (SCO).

See refers to the usage of Forescout for visibility.

Control refers to the ability to restrict access for endpoints.

Orchestrate refers to the ability to integrate with various third party platforms.

When grouping the policy families with the architecture breakdown, the See phase encompasses Discover, Classify and Assess, the control policy family covers Control, and Orchestrate would be covered by additional policies.

In the newer professional services policy set, the policies use a structured group configuration, so it is necessary to import the groups first, in order to maintain the correct structure.

Let's step through these policy families individually.

Discover (1 policy)

The discover Policy covers the primary classification. The Professional services policy is similar to the template for Classification, with some tuning based on feedback from the Forescout professional services team. At a high level, the Discover policy sorts devices into major device types, such as Windows, Printers, VoIP, Mobile, Linux, and a few others. The policy adds these various category devices to groups, to be used in later policies.

Classify (4-10 policies)

The classify policy builds on the groupings made in the discover policy and further sorts the endpoints. Typically the major groups will each have their own policy. Some of the common classify policies are Windows classification, Linux classification, and Macintosh Classification. The classification policy takes the group of endpoints from the discover policy and sorts them further, typically focusing on manageability. For example, the Windows classification policy sorts the devices that were added to the Windows group and sorts them into managed and unmanaged. Managed devices are added to respective groups in order to further check them against additional policies in the assess section. Depending on the customer environment, unmanaged devices may be left alone, or may be added to a group for restriction, quarantine or being blocked from the network altogether.

Notice that I said 4-10 policies. Although there are a few included with the professional services policy set, some customers choose to add additional   policies for some of the other device types. For example, perhaps an organization has printers that are managed by SNMP. A printer classification policy could be written to see which printers were manageable by attempting a SNMP read using the relevant SNMP user or community.

Assess (4-10 policies)

For devices that are manageable (such as Managed windows endpoints), here we progress to additional policies to check the manageable devices against additional policies, typically based on the organizations Acceptable Use Policies (AUP) or on other expected items. These are often also called compliance policies.

Sample Assess policies may include the following:

Checking for running and updated Antivirus software

Checking for disk encryption on Windows endpoints

Checking for the organizations Security suite software

Checking for various patch agents

Checking for disallowed applications (peer to peer, instant messenger Apps, etc)

Checking endpoints for old software versions (such as Java or Flash)

Endpoints that are not considered compliant, due to not matching what they should may be added to groups to either remediate or quarantine them later.

Control (0-3 policies)

Control policies are typically where restrictions are placed.

On the wired network side, possible restrictions could be changing to a restricted, quarantine, or guest VLAN, applying ACLs, or even shutting down switchports to block an endpoint from the network.

On the wireless side, there may be wireless restrictions, including wireless role changes or ACL applying, depending on vendor, or blocking an endpoint from associating to the wireless.

Additionally, control policies may include items like guest registration with internet only access.

Notice that I said zero to three policies typically. Zero because some customers start with just visibility and some customers are only interested in visibility. While basic visibility can be achieved quite quickly, implementating control typically may take a bit of planning. If you are using VLAN changes for example, the alternate VLANs need to be provisioned throughout the network. If using ACLs for restricting, there typically is some amount of testing of the ACLs to make sure there are as few unexpected issues as possible.

There are a several additional policies included with the professional services policy set, mostly additional samples showing some of the functionality.

There are a few additional policy folders potentially included, depending on your particular version of the professional services policy set.

Some of the common groupings are 'Informational', 'Security', and 'Test'.

Informational policies are typically used to validate whether the plugins are operating correctly. For example, the Switch Integration Audit policy is used to highlight potential misconfigurations in the switch plugin. If the final goal is control, you will need to have visibility of where and how the endpoints are connected before you will be able to restrict them.

Security policies may be used to sweep the environment for potential security vulnerabilities. Typically, these would be items created from the templates that are available from the Security Policy Templates module.

Test policies is a common folder to use as a placeholder for testing policies in a limited capacity before rolling out to the whole organization.

9. Windows Manageability

In this chapter we will be taking a look at the options available for Windows management.

When it comes down to managing Windows assets, the biggest question is whether to use a service account or the SecureConnector agent. While we covered some of the configuration options earlier in the HPS Inspection engine portion of the Options menu, in this section we will take a look at the high level overview of both of these methods.

Windows Service Account

This account will need to be an account that has administrative access on the endpoints that you wish to manage. If you have multiple domains, you may need to have one for each domain, unless there is a trust relationship between the domains. Additional specifics regarding individual permissions needed for login, DCOM settings, etc. can be found in the HPS Inspection Engine help file Appendix. In some cases, if existing groups that have administrative access to the endpoint are not used, then group policy would need to be pushed out to tell the endpoints that this account should have administrative access on the endpoint. Additionally, if precautions are not taken, this account also runs the risk of potentially getting locked out, which would make devices appear as unmanaged. The service account uses WMI or Remote Registry to connect, and also uses SMB. In the event there are ACLs or firewalls in the path between the appliances and the endpoints, those firewalls will need to allow access to those protocols. Additionally, there are also third party integrations through eyeExtend for things like integrating with CyberArk for password locker functionality.

Note: If you change the password, that by itself is not sufficient for policies to be evaluated against the host the same as a recheck. Typically, if you change the password, you will want to recheck the devices that are not showing as managed, otherwise you could just wait until the next recheck interval.

HTTP Localhost Login

While this is rarely used, there is also an option called HTTP localhost login. With this configuration, you ask the user for credentials that you then use to evaluate their endpoint.   This action is under the action group of Manage and also updates the property Host Manageable (Local).

SecureConnector

SecureConnector is a small lightweight agent which establishes a management connection to the endpoint's managing appliance and is used as a connection mechanism for queries t

As it is a small agent installed on the endpoint, it is not dependent on the endpoint being a member of the Domain.   It can be used on machines that are not domain members, which could be devices managed by a third party or devices which are configured in workgroups or even guests or contractors.

Re-homing

In the event that the managing appliance is unavailable, the agent will attempt to establish a connection to the EM and then to the Recovery Manager, and then any additional appliances listed in the HPS Inspection Engine SecureConnector tab entries for "additional appliance connections".

SC Installation Types

There are three install types.

- Install as an application
- Install as a service
- Install dissolvable

Install as Application

This method installs as an application and runs in the user context. It will not be running if there is not a user logged in.

Install as Service

Installing as a service runs in the system context and is still running even if a user is not logged in. In most cases, this is considered the recommended approach.

Install Dissolvable

Dissolvable runs in memory. This could be used to temporarily place on guest or contractor machines (or BYOD machines) in order to do basic compliance checks.

Agent Deployment

The SC agent can be downloaded from any appliance or EM, but it is recommended to download from the EM. Selections to make include items such as installation type, whether or not to show the system tray icon. These flags are included in the file name, so make sure to not rename it. It can be deployed as part of a software image if imaging is used in the environment, or via software deployment software. It can also be installed from a network file share or emailed or saved to a CD or other removable media. Additionally, the agent can be pushed from the appliance itself, either by HTTP action or by administrative permissions, if you have an HPS service account with administrative access.

Note: Some organizations may not want to use a service account long-term, but may be OK with having one temporarily. One deployment option would be to add a service account, use it to push the SecureConnector agent out to endpoints, and then remove the service account from the HPS Inspection plugin.

Secure Connector Actions

Do you want the agent to show on the Windows desktop in the system tray? If you wish to use the SecureConnector "balloon message" as an action, showing the system tray icon is a requirement.

Additionally, the actions 'disable dual homed', 'disable external devices' also require SecureConnector to be installed. It is also possible to install temporarily just in order to perform one of these specific actions.

Event Driven Monitoring

One of the additional features that SecureConnector provides is a feature called Event Driven Monitoring. For certain properties such as services or External Devices, these will result in a triggered update being forwarded to the managing appliance if there is a change. With a policy checking for USB external devices, a service account will only match if the device is connected at the time that the policy runs or when a recheck is running. With event driven monitoring, a new USB device being plugged in would forward a triggered update.

Note: Although it may not be a common configuration, one possible configuration is that an appliance could be configured in an internet-facing DMZ and remote worker machines could establish a connection to the appliance, even if the machines were not connected to a VPN connection to the organization.

Service account or SecureConnector

Some organizations choose service account purely due to an aversion to agents. Some organizations have several agents already on the endpoint and don't want any more, no matter how nonintrusive they are.

Sometimes the directionality can affect the decision. With a service account, the connection is established from the appliance towards the endpoint. With SecureConnector, the connection is initiated from the endpoint towards the appliance.

Some organizations take a hybrid approach, and use service accounts when possible, while also using the SecureConnector agent for hosts not on the domain.

Some organizations take the 'belt and suspenders' approach, and use both service accounts and service accounts at the same time, so that there is a backup method to manage the endpoint.

Regardless which method of the two you use, for most compliance policies, hosts need to be managed to be properly evaluated against compliance policies (discussed in the next chapter)

10. Compliance

In this chapter we will be taking a look at some of the considerations with regards to compliance, sample types of items checked, and approaches to remediating items found noncompliant.

Compliance Considerations

For most organizations, the initial breakdown of devices during the Discovery policy and the Classification breakdown between determination of managed vs unmanaged is pretty consistent.

When it comes to assessing for compliance, however, there is a much wider variety of what sort of items different organizations want to check for compliance.

The Forescout Professional Services policy set gives a variety of examples, but typically they will need some tuning for individual environments. The current set refers to the category as 'Assess' instead of 'Compliance', but the specific items checked are the same.

Sample compliance checks:

- Checking Antivirus agent software is running
- Checking Antivirus software is up to date
- Check various other third party Agents - Patch software

- Check endpoint firewall software
- Check disk encryption status
- Check for file shares on endpoints
- Check for undesired software (P2P, IM, cloud storage)
- Windows Patch Checking
- Windows USB external device checking
- Checking for specific versions of software
- Checking for old versions of software (such as Java)
- Other custom checks via script
- Other checks via SPT template

Additional questions that you should be able to answer that may guide you to what types of compliance policies and how many you want in your organization:

What is the organization's AUP (Acceptable Use Policy)?

Are the compliance policies different for different device types?

Are both servers and workstations in scope? If so, do they have the same checks being performed?

Do laptops have the same compliance checks as desktops?

If something doesn't match the expected compliance, what actions to take?

Is the intention to remediate in place?

Is the intention to restrict access while remediating?

What notifications to send and how? Syslog? Email? HTTP Notification? Send to SIEM?

Notify admin or the end user?

If AV, typically not much point to notify user. If P2P or IM, may want to send user a warning message or HTTP notification

If multiple remediations are needed, are the remediations handled in separate policies, or one single policy handling multiple remediations with different subrules, so that remediations are not attempted concurrently?

Windows Compliance Policies

Typically the Main Rule condition will be 'Member of Group - Managed Windows Devices'. If the endpoints aren't managed, then the checks for things like processes, services or being able to run scripts on the Windows endpoint will be unsuccessful.

Because subrules are processed top down, the subrule for your compliant devices typically will be first, so that the majority of your devices aren't checked against multiple rules.

In theory, most of your hosts should be compliant. In general, a sub rule matching a non-compliant device will have a more frequent recheck. Optionally, specify a recheck host action as part of your remediation.

Windows patch checking

Forescout has a mechanism for checking Microsoft patches on managed Windows machines. While it can be quite effective, it may not be the best option for larger deployments.

Typically a larger organization may have an existing software platform handling patch distribution. Whether that is something like BigFix, SCCM, or ePO or some other product, in many cases it may be easier to integrate with those platforms, rather than running scripts on the endpoints to recheck items that another platform is already checking.

The default method uses Microsoft's offline scan file, which at the time of this writing is several hundred Megabytes. Pushing a large file around the enterprise may not be an issue if appliances are located at individual sites, however it can have negative impact on bandwidth if this is being pushed across slower wan links. Enabling this functionality inadvertently can have deleterious impact on the environment, as it can saturate WAN links if not careful.

There are some configuration options which can reduce the bandwidth used, either by distributing the file in advance to the endpoints, or by selectively choosing to not push the file for specific endpoint IP ranges (such as remote offices) and instead just querying those endpoints directly and asking the endpoint what patches it is missing.

One other point of complexity for the patch checking mechanism is that some environments may choose to exclude certain patches from deployment, possibly due to issues found in the organization when testing that patch. So it would still show up as a critical patch missing, even though the the "organization approved" patches may be at 100% installed.

In the event that the organization has one of the other patch management platforms in place, the most common is to use Forescout to check the health/presence of that agent software as a compliance check. Some will use an integration to also query the patch management platform, and some will have

Forescout perform the patch checking in parallel, as a "second set of eyes".

Remediation Locations

Some choose to perform within the same policy, or within a separate single policy.

When dealing with multiple compliance policies, one option is to remediate within the individual policies and another option is to remediate in a separate single policy that does remediations for multiple compliance policies. Typically this would be handled with adding to a group for the remediation item, and then matching that group in a later policy.

The following are questions that you may need to consider when deciding between the two

What are your remediation actions? Are you starting services, installing software, or just notifying the help desk or other group that is manually intervening to remediate.

If you are doing multiple installs, you may want to have the compliance policies do an add to group, and have a later policy use that group as scope or main rule and do the remediation. It is also possible that depending on the specific installers, it may be better to do them one at a time, rather than potentially having two installers running at the same time on the same endpoint.

Having remediations handled in a separate single policy can also be easier from an operational visibility perspective. Sometimes it's easiest for an operations group to look at a single policy, where they can see which hosts match the policy and which remediation a host is currently receiving. Additionally, if each remediation has it's own sub rule, any installs will be sequential rather than concurrent, due to the top down nature of matching sub rules one by one.

One other question that comes up is whether to leave devices in place while remediating versus moving to a limited access location via ACL or VLAN change that only has access to the patching servers.

Whitelisting / Blacklisting

Whitelisting is the process of listing allowed programs and checking against a list. Blacklisting is the process of listing programs that should not be running. While Forescout technically can do both, in general whitelisting may not be very practical due to the large number of applications in the environment. If you have a smaller environment and a short list of programs, then whitelisting may be possible.

11. Control

In this chapter, we will go over the principles of control.

Getting to Control

In the world of real estate, there's a common saying that you may have heard, "location, location, location". When it comes to the world of Forescout, what matters most is "visibility, visibility, visibility".

Control is typically the end goal, but if you don't have a solid foundation of visibility, then restrictions made will not have optimal efficacy.

In most cases, it is recommended that when you start your deployment, you start with just visibility, and don't move on to control until you have monitored and tuned the Forescout platform for your environment.

Even though we recommend starting with visibility, control policy framework can still be built out at the time of initial install. Many customers purchase Forescout Professional Services as part of the hardware purchase. Depending on how much professional service time they have purchased, it may be used in a single visit, or at various stages of the project deployment.

The usage of keywords 'framework' or 'staging' is important here. The policy can be built out however leaving the control actions disabled initially, maintaining the remaining logic for main rules and sub rules. This allows the visibility of seeing 'who WOULD be restricted' without actually restricting the endpoints. It is important to monitor carefully before enabling the actions, as specific use cases in your environment may not have been accommodated.

At a high level, control is used to provide a restriction. This could be an ACL action, a VLAN change, a Wireless restriction, a switch or wireless block action, or a VPN disconnection. Whichever method is used, at a high level, the control is a restriction taken that modifies the network infrastructure, so having the visibility of HOW the device is connected is essential.

Common Control Policies
- Restrict Wired Guest users to a VLAN that only allows internet access
- Restrict Managed devices missing patches to a Remediation network
- Restrict infected devices to a Quarantine network
- Restrict certain devices to a "no access" VLAN
- Block Unknown Devices
- Restrict Guest Endpoints from the internal wired network

While 'Block Unknown Devices' may sound straightforward, in most cases there is additional complexity, due to inability to give tangible criteria of what defines a device as 'unknown'.

Sample Unknown Device Discussion

During a discussion with a customer, they stated that they wanted to restrict employees from bringing in their own computers. When asked how new computers were provisioned and onboarded, they said that someone at the office would go down to the local computer shop and buy a computer and bring it in and connect it to the network. Based on this information, there was no clear delineation between the two, and it was expressed to them that it would be very difficult to determine 'unknown', with this particular process.

How Many Policies

While an organization may have a large number of compliance policies, typically there are just a few control policies. Since control is based on how someone is connected to the network, there are usually only a few different options. Typically the flow is to have a variety of policies that populate groups within Forescout which the control policies then use as scope.

For example, it is common for organizations to have classification policies for Linux, Macintosh, Windows. Each of these classification policies may have unknown devices. If one of the desired objectives is to have a control policy to block unknown devices, then each of these subrules – Unknown Linux, Unknown Macintosh, and Unknown Windows could have an additional action of adding to a group "Unknown Devices" to be later referenced by a single control policy.

One control policy can be used to perform multiple control actions, with different subrules for the individual actions.

Utilizing a single policy for control can also be easier for operational staff to have a single place to look in order to see who is being restricted by the platform. As mentioned earlier, within a policy, sub rules are processed top down. In general, it is recommended practice within a control policy to include at the top of the list one or more subrules for devices that should be exempted from control. If devices may match more than one restriction, such as matching criteria for quarantine, remediation, and blocking, you will also want to order your sub rules from most restrictive to least restrictive.

Sample Control Policy Logic

Here we are going to look at sample logic for a control policy for endpoints connected to switches. If you also have wireless devices being restricted, you could add additional subrules for restricting by wireless actions, such as wireless block and wireless role changes. For VPN connected devices, you could use VPN block or potentially Virtual Firewall as an action.

Policy Name 1.2 Switchport Control

Scope: All Ips

Main Rule:

      Condition – One is True

            Member of Group Blocked Hosts

            Member of Group Quarantine Hosts

            Member of Group Remediation Hosts

Sub Rule 1

      Name – Exempt from Control

      Condition

            Member of Group – Control Exemption

Sub Rule 2

    Name - Unknown Switch

    Condition - All are False

        Switch IP - Any

Sub Rule 3

    Condition - All are true

        Member of Group Blocked Hosts

    Action - Switchport Block

    Action - Send Message to Syslog

Sub Rule 4

    Condition - One is True

        Member of Group - Quarantine Hosts

    Action - Add to VLAN - Quarantine

    Action - Send Message to Syslog

Sub Rule 5

    Condition - One is True

        Member of Group - Remediation Hosts

    Action - Add to VLAN - Remediation

    Action - Send Message to Syslog

Notifications

If restricting a host, it's common practice to send out a notification. While it's obviously not practical to send a notification to an end use that you kicked off the network, typically notifications would be sent to a logging or SIEM platform, or potentially select notifications via email to an administrator group.

12. Advanced Policy Concepts

In this chapter we will be discussing a variety of additional policy concepts.

Default Groups

We have two specialty groups as defaults within the Forescout platform: 'Properties - Passive Learning' and 'Ignored IPs'

For the Passive Learning group, devices are still processed against policy, however no active property information is gathered. Active property information is information that is learned by directly querying an endpoint. So, learning about the switchport or processing traffic seen in SPAN or tap sessions on channels are considered passive, but directly querying a host to check if a TCP port is open or attempting to log in to a windows machine with a service account would be active inspection.

The 'Ignored IPs' group is treated specially as well. For devices in the 'Ignored IPs' group, the Discovery and Inventory policies under Options are still processed, but the endpoints are excluded from being matched by any of the Policy Manager policies.

153

SPT

The Security Policy Templates is a content module that includes various sample policy templates.

These templates are to identify devices that may be vulnerable to various threats. Some may be device vulnerabilities specific to certain software versions which can be detected. Some templates also can be used to investigate looking for known compromised devices. These can exclude things like certain ransomware software infections. Once the module is installed, the policy templates can be found under the "Vulnerability and Response" portion of the policy wizard. Some of the policies are using basic checks, others use scripts that may be run against the endpoints from the appliance, or in some cases are scripts that are run on managed endpoints directly. As new vulnerabilities arise, there are new versions of the plugin available to cover recently learned vulnerabilities.

Dashboard Policies

The dashboard policy template creates a number of policies which will be used to populate the default dashboard widgets. If you don't run this template, some of the the dashboard widgets will not have data populated.

Appliance Health

Newer versions of the Tech-support plugin include sample policies to monitor the health of the Forescout appliances themselves, including checking for resource consumption, policy consumption.

Other plugin updates sometimes will also include additional policy templates relevant to that plugin.

Reviewing Policy Components

In our earlier chapters, we discussed the main portions of a policy.

Name

Scope

Main Rule

 Conditions (optional) and Actions (optional)

Sub Rule(s)

 Conditions (optional) and Actions (optional)

Let's review these and expand on the earlier definitions that we started with.

Scope

In the simplified explanation, we defined scope as just an address range. However, we can refine the scope further. Under the scope section when creating a policy, or when selecting the edit button next to the scope when editing a policy, if you look closely under the segment / address list, you will notice two wrenches or spanners. Clicking on the one on the right with the small cog or gear will bring up the advanced view, where we can see additional options for filter and exceptions. Filter allows you to select a group, and ONLY endpoints matching the specified group(s) will be evaluated against. Exceptions allows you to exclude by IP address, MAC address, Netbios hostname, user name, or groups. Under the basic view, there are no filters or exceptions.

If you import a policy and the segment ranges defined in the scope do not match your defined segment structure, then the policy will be imported with NO scope. No scope is different than "no conditions" for a main rule. No scope means that NO endpoints will match the policy.

Main Rule

The Main rule has additional options as well. At the bottom of the main rule is an advanced section. We can adjust the timer for the specific policy rechecks. You can change to check more frequently or less frequently, to only check if specific admission events are seen. Additionally on the General tab, you can also adjust timers for Ignore information and the Admission resolve delay. The default is for these to follow the global timers under the Options menu. Additionally, you also have the ability to set main rule exceptions for IP, MAC, NetBIOS hostname, User names, and groups.

For the Admission resolve delay, one example of an increased value would be if you were checking for a program that took extra time to start up when a machine started. One customer had a patching program that took up to 5 minutes to fully start up when a workstation first came online. By setting a higher value for just this policy, they were able to ensure that the policy checks were more accurate.

Sub Rule

Additionally sub-rules also have an option to adjust the timers and whether to recheck matching hosts on an admission.

As an example, for a policy that is looking for Antivirus, you may check a subrule more frequently for the devices that are out of date for their AV definitions, whereas for devices that are up to date, you might not need to check as frequently.

From a best practices perspective, short simple policies are typically recommended. In general, most policies will have less than 20 subrules, and most will have less than 10.

Typically, we start with the Discovery and Classify families as discussed in the Policy set chapter to break the endpoints into smaller groups. Initially, these policies are just sorting into smaller groups.

In most cases, the last subrule has a condition of "no conditions" and will therefore match any endpoints that have made it to that point. Additionally, if you add a subrule, it gets added at the very end. If your previous "last subrule" has a condition of 'no conditions', your new sub rule below that will never match anything. So if you add a subrule, you typically will want to bring it higher in the list of subrules, at least above the last rule and sometimes much higher.

Just like main rules, sub rules also have the option to set exceptions under the advanced tab for IP addresses, MAC addresses, NetBIOS Hostname, User Name and Group. If you set criteria for an exception, then that particular endpoint will skip that subrule in the processing and continue processing against the next subrule.

Condition criteria

Similarly to the options discussed for advanced view for scope, if you look to the right side for the condition section for a main rule or subrule you will see two wrenches/spanners, and the one on the left is for basic view and the one on the right for advanced view.

In the basic view you have the following options:

- One is true
- One is False
- All are True
- All are False

Under the advanced view, you can get into much more complex boolean logic, including parenthesis and not and and/or logic. In general, be careful when using more complex logic, and validate your results.

Additional Condition logic

When checking an individual property, you have additional options for matching that specific property. For most properties there will be two radio buttons at the top, the first being "Meets the criteria" and the second "Does not meet the criteria"

For "Member of Group" you will see a list of groups as seen in your group hierarchy.

For other items, you may see a drop-down list with the following entries:

- Any Value
- Contains
- Starts With
- Ends With
- In List
- Matches
- Matches Expression

For items that may change or may be referenced in multiple policies, the option 'In List' can be useful because you can just update the list instead of updating each of the individual policies.

Note: Do not confuse 'Device Information - Member of Group' with 'User Directory - Member of'. The first one refers to the groups within Forescout, whereas the second one is for groups within a User Directory server, such as Active Directory groups that a user is a member of.

Additionally, there may be a checkbox selection for 'Match case'. If you want a case-sensitive match, make sure to check the box.

Irresolvable

For some properties, such as Windows services or DNS name, we have a checkbox item for 'Evaluate irresolvable criteria as' which also has a drop down box for 'True or False'

Forgetting to make a selection for the checkbox can cause hosts to be stuck in an irresolvable state, and they won't continue policy processing to the next subrule.

You will always want that checkbox selected for properties where it is available, and more than 95% of the time, you will want the dropdown selection to be false, so it will read 'Evaluate irresolvable criteria as False'. The reason for setting this to False in most cases is to assume the worst-case scenario. So if for some reason you are unable to resolve a list of services on an endpoint, you may want to assume that the specific service that you are looking for is not there. Selecting irresolvable as false means that the condition will not match. If this is a condition on the main rule, the endpoint would not match the policy. If this is a condition on a subrule, typically that would result in the endpoint then being checked against the next subrule.

There is a global setting that can override this, under Options-Advanced-Policy, but in general, you will want to keep that setting under options as 'According to user-defined settings per property'.

As a general rule, properties that have the 'Evaluate Irresolvable' checkbox available are ones that are resolved externally to Forescout. Some examples are DNS name,

Windows services and processes, patch and antivirus status. For internal properties such as 'Member of group' which corresponds to a group within Forescout, or 'IP address', these items don't have the checkbox available.

One use case for "irresolvable as True" is commonly seen in some cases when checking the AV update date in compliance policies. Since the condition is 'AV update older than', a setting of true would assume the worst case, which would be that the AV update is old when the date can not be determined.

Another example for 'irresolvable as true' can be in order to identify irresolvable devices early in a policy, rather than having multiple sub rules time out when they aren't going to resolve. For example, if looking for a service, you can look for a dummy service that would never really exist, such as 'manamana' with 'irresolvable as true'. As a result, the only ones that would match that subrule would be ones that were truly irresolvable.

Policy Testing

In most cases it is recommended to test new policies on a small subset of endpoints. In some cases it could be a single endpoint, a specific range of addresses, or perhaps a single location. After testing is completed on the small subset, expand to other areas.

If additional testing is to be done for significant changes to an existing policy, typically this would start with duplicating the policy, and then setting the scope to a small subset of endpoints for the additional testing.

Policy Rollout

After the initial testing, typically policies are rolled out to larger groups. In some cases policies are rolled out across the environment all at once. In other cases, policies may be rolled out to certain groups of sites by region. If rolling out to specific regions, including a branch in your segment hierarchy for region can help facilitate this scoping, and then you can match by that branch, rather than matching the individual locations.

Function vs Network Function

Network function is the older method, which is primarily derived from older methods such as poF and NMAP fingerprinting. Function is the newer property which utilizes additional logic within the Device Classification Engine plugin, which uses the content information from the Device Profile Library.

Property Source

As mentioned earlier in the switch section, the same property can be learned from multiple sources. MAC addresses, for example, can be learned from the switch plugin, from DHCP and ARP replies seen in the channel traffic, from NetBIOS query, from SecureConnector clients, from Wireless Controllers, and so on. Hovering on the value in the details pane from the main home tab will show where the value was learned from (and when).

Policy Flow

On the All Polices tab of the Details pane, as mentioned earlier you can see the Matched or Unmatched for each policy. If you have 30 policies, a host most likely will not match all of them. To the right of the Matched/Unmatched line listing the policy name is an underlined link for 'View Policy Flow'. This will give you a graphical view of the policies and policy subrules that matched in order for a host to match a specific policy. For example if you have a device being remediated, you can expand to see the entire flow from initial classification in the Discovery policy, to the Classification policy determining manageability, to the Assess policy evaluating compliance, and finally to the remediation policy.

View Troubleshooting Messages

As mentioned earlier, with the home tab selected, the host line you have selected in the top detections tab will have their details shown below in the details pane.

On the far right of the Details pane is a small letter 'i' in a circle. If you hover, it will say 'show troubleshooting messages'. Depending which tab you have selected you will see additional information about certain properties. If you have the endpoint 'profile' tab selected, it will show various source information, showing how certain properties were resolved, such as by the NetBIOS plugin (NBTscan) or DHCP, and so on.

Show All Details

Just to the left of the 'view troubleshooting messages' button above, is the 'Show all details' button, which if not selected looks like a double arrow pointing downward. It will expand out all items in the details pane. For example, if you have the

'All Policies' tab selected, it will expand out and show all main rules and sub rules.

Action Families
Initially, our policies focused on the "Add to Group" action as we were just sorting into smaller groups of devices. As we move on to more granular groups, we typically will want to perform additional actions. Perhaps we want to send some sort of notification, such as a syslog message or an email, sometimes we may want to perform a restrictive action such as a switchport ACL or VLAN change, or possibly an action such as an Antivirus update. For now, let's talk through these various action families and cover some of the most common for each.

The primary seven action families are:
- Audit
- Authenticate
- Classify
- Manage
- Notify
- Remediate
- Restrict

In addition, some of the additional modules have their own group added for just that module.

Audit
Mostly used for logging, here you will find the options for syslog, CEF, DEX web request, DEX update External database.

Additionally, if you have added a SIEM module, you may see that here as well, such as send update to QRadar

Authenticate

Items under this grouping are HTTP login and HTTP Log Out. HTTP Login is used for Guest Registration. HTTP Log Out can be used if you need to log someone out based on them meeting specific criteria

Classify

Classify allows you to manually classify Function, Network Function, OS Classification, or Vendor and Model Classification. Overwriting the classifications due to defined criteria allows you to classify devices that may not be properly classified automatically by the Forescout software.

Manage

Some of the items here are for managing additional specific endpoint properties, such as labels, groups, counters and lists. Additionally some are for items such as starting, stopping, and upgrading SecureConnector. One action that we discussed earlier was the action "add to group". The Add to group action also has an additional option to "expire when host no longer matches". So for policies such as the policy we created from the primary classification template, we have this item selected for the add to group actions. So if a Windows no longer matches our subrule for Windows, we will dynamically remove it from the Windows group, and it would no longer match subsequent policies which use the Windows group as scoping.

Notify

Notify covers various other methods of notification, such as email, HTTP notifications, balloon notifications through SecureConnector. When dealing with notification items, one of the topics for discussion is the usage of tags. Tags are used to display property values of an endpoint. For an example, the default subject line for an email is 'CounterACT: Event at {ip}'. In this case, the tag {ip} is replaced when the email gets send out by the corresponding database value for that property for the endpoint. If you click in the Subject or Body portion of an Notify-Send Email action that you are configuring, you can click on the "Add Tags" button to see the tags that are available based on the plugins and modules that you have installed in your environment.

Remediate

Remediate actions include a variety of actions many of which are executed directly on the endpoints. Running scripts on endpoints, killing processes, start updates for antivirus, SCCM or OS are some of the options here.

The actions "disable dual homed, disable external devices" require SecureConnector to be installed.

Restrict

Restrict items are mostly actions applied at the network infrastructure to restrict a device. Switchport block, ACL restrictions, VLAN changes, 802.1x changes to authorization, wireless restrictions or blocking.

Action scheduling

The default is for an action to occur once at the time the main rule or sub rule which has the action is matched. Sometimes you may want to delay the action, sometimes you may want the action to recur. Or, you may want the action to end after a specific time.

In addition to scheduling, you could also configure multiple actions on the same main rule or subrule. For example, a policy checking Managed Windows devices for Antivirus could have a subrule matching devices with AV not updated with the following three actions

1. Update Antivirus

   Start immediately, every 10 minutes, end after 3 occurrences

2. Recheck Host

   Wait for 15 minutes, every 15 minutes, end after 3 occurrences

3. Send email

   Wait for 1 hour, send once

If the device properly receives its updates, and no longer matches the subrule after the recheck, but before 1 hour has passed, it will no longer match the policy and the email will not send. In this example, we are attempting the remediation first, and then sending the notification only if the remediation doesn't work.

In the case of a direct restrictive action, such as an ACL applied or being blocked from the network, you may want to send out the notification at the same time as the restriction.

Custom / Comparison properties

Under the policy manager, there is the functionality to create custom properties or a custom comparison property to compare two existing properties, and take differing policy decisions based on whether the properties match or not. These are not commonly used, but at times they could be used for specific cases. If you create a custom property, it will then appear in the conditions section for main rules and subrules. If you create a comparison property, it will appear under Comparison Properties and the selection options are a checkbox list including: both unknown, values are identical, values differ, or one or other are irresolvable, with top radio dial buttons for Meets the following or Does not meet the following.

Policy Categorization

In order for policies to be considered 'compliance' policies and show on the compliance tab for a host. Under the policy manager page, select the policy main rule and the 'Categorize' button on the right side. From the drop down select Compliance as the categorization, and then for each subrule select one of the labels: Unlabeled, Compliant, Not Compliant, Manageable, or NotManageable. In most cases you will just use 'Compliant' or 'Not Compliant' for the individual subrules.

There are also categorizations for Corporate/Guest and Classification. One policy can be categorized as a 'Classification' policy.

The power of scripting

Scripting can be a very powerful tool. In most cases we are talking about running a script against a managed workstation. Sometimes there are scripts provided by a vendor in order to test something like a client installation. In other cases, it may just be a basic script to gather an additional property. Although we say 'script' it can either be a script file or a single line command. If you are using a single line command, you may have additional parsing to restrict your output. Sometimes making a basic script file is a bit cleaner from the way it looks in the GUI.

Scripts are stored in the scripts repository folder. When you upload a script to the EM, it gets pushed to all appliances. Additionally, some of the built-in property checks use scripts to resolve. The exact folders are slightly different for built in scripts versus scripts that you upload, so don't worry if you don't see all the scripts in the list.

People often ask what the available extensions are for script files. The short answer is that for the most part Forescout doesn't care what the script extension is. The endpoint where you are running the script is the one that needs to understand how to run the script. Whether that is a .sh script on Linux or

MAC, or a .bat or .exe, Forescout just pushes the file to the endpoint and executes it on the endpoint.

For larger files, for example larger software packages, it is recommended to use a network file path to a network share which the endpoints have access. It is not recommended to push around large files, and in some cases, adding large files to the scripts folder can cause issues with communication between EM and appliances.

Scripts can be run both as CONDITIONS and as ACTIONS. For example, checking for serial number (example later in this chapter) is typically done as a CONDITION script, using the condition "Windows Script Result". Whereas, a script for updating Antivirus, would be a script done as an ACTION. Scripts done as an action are most common when trying to fix or remediate something. For CONDITION scripts, those can be added as a column within the GUI. Just click on the top column bar and select 'Add Column', and you can type 'Script Result' in the upper left search box, and then add the column specific to your script.

In almost all cases, your scripts will be what is called 'noninteractive'. The user doesn't need to see a pop-up box for something you are doing in the background. In the rare event a specific script requires that it be run interactively, make sure that you select that checkbox where you are running that script.

Example - Condition Script - Serial Number - WMI Query

Serial number can be pulled from a WMI query. This can be done with a single line command. For example, you could use the command 'wmic bios get serialnumber', although the output will also include a line of the text 'SerialNumber'. If you want that text to not be returned, you can filter further using the Windows 'findstr' and use the command 'wmic bios get serialnumber | findstr -v SerialNumber' to exclude the line of text. We mentioned early in our policy discussion that we could just exclude subrules as they are optional. In this case, since there is just one item that we are looking for, we can look for the item in the main rule. In order to set this up, we can set our Scope to the desired IP range and add an additional scope filter of the 'Managed Windows' group. Then in the main rule, we could just set the condition "Windows Expected Script Result" and use the command 'wmic bios get serialnumber | findstr -v SerialNumber' and the dropdown of "Any Value". Additionally, by using the "Expected Script Result", you can also add the item as a column in the GUI. For something like Serial number, this might be something worthwhile to have as a column for things like an inventory report.

Example - Action Script - Client Install

For agent software such as SMS/SCCM, there is a small installer that will point the endpoint at a server in order to download additional client software. In this case, CCMSetup.exe is the name of the small file. Configuration items such as the management point, fallback status point, and sitecode can be specified on the same line, or on a specially formatted file.

```
CCMSetup.exe /mp:SMSMP01 /logon SMSSITECODE=S01
FSP=SMSFSP01
```

```
CCMSetup.exe /config:"configurationFile.txt"
```

The problem with the second option is that we don't have the configurationfile.txt file on the endpoint. Referencing a file that doesn't exist won't get us the correct results. In this case, we can get around this by using the run script action. We can run two script actions with a scheduled delay on the second file. For the first one, we can just set configurationFile.txt as the 'script'. Although the text file doesn't execute the same way as an exe or a bat file, selecting it as a script to run will still allow Forescout to push the file to the temporary directory. Then after a slight delay (5 or 10 seconds is typically sufficient), when you run the installer file, the txt file will still be in the temporary directory, and it can be used by the setup file referencing it.

Other installers may have a similar properties or configuration file and using this mechanism to pre-push the file can be easier than writing a larger batch file that retrieves the file within the script from an external file location.

HTTP actions / Guest Registration
The primary HTTP actions are HTTP login, HTTP redirection, HTTP Notification.

Typically, these are handled by seeing an HTTP GET request in the channel traffic and sending an HTTP 302 Redirect to redirect the web session to the appliance. Optionally it can be redirected via the DNS enforce functionality, which is discussed in another chapter.

Note: If the device is managed device by either service account or SecureConnector, you can use the management connection to attempt to open a browser, without waiting to see web traffic to redirect, utilizing the checkbox "Attempt to open the endpoint browser" (Exact wording varies slightly between the different actions).

In order to implement the guest registration functionality, from a minimalist perspective, you just need to configure a policy or policies to determine what hosts you consider as guests, and to configure the subrule action for HTTP login. However, there are still several questions that you need to decide. Below are some of the typical questions related to guest registration configuration.

Who should be sent to guest registration?

> All unmanaged devices?

> Just specific devices?

Guest registration options

> Require validation by email or phone?

Require a sponsor?

Require Terms and Conditions?

Are internal users able to log in with corporate credentials?

How log is registration valid for?

How often do they need to log in?

Traffic restricted while waiting to register?

Are any traffic flows still allowed?

Restricted how? - Virtual Firewall, ACL, VLAN change?

Confirmation Identifiers

When dealing with HTTP Notifications, there is the concept of a text-based field called a confirmation identifier. You can set a specific confirmation identifier value on the HTTP Notification action, and then can match that same identifier in another policy, if you want to check for the condition that the person actually clicked the button at the bottom of the HTTP notification.

Common Credentials

Forescout provides policy templates to check for default/commonly used credentials for telnet/SSH and SNMP. Additionally, you can add to the list under Options - IoT Posture Assessment Engine. The policy templates are located under IoT Posture Assessment in the policy list, and there are separate policies for telnet, SSH, and SNMP.

Case Study - Matching the Passive Group

One of the special default groups within Forescout that we talked about earlier was the 'Properties - Passive Learning' group. There may be times when you may want to match the passive group for a subrule exception.

By default, you cannot select this group as an exception, however there is a workaround available, however it requires some manual editing.

Configure a new policy with match group as a condition, using one of your existing groups to match. Configure the action of 'Add to Group' and create a new group. Call this new group something else, such as 'My Passive Group'.

Next, export the policy and edit the match group condition in the XML file to match the group identifier for the 'Properties - Passive Learning' group. The id for the Passive Learning group is '-2'

PARAM NAME="group-name" VALUE="id:-2;name:Properties - Passive Learning"

Now delete the policy in policy Manager, and then import your edited policy and apply the changes.

Now your newly created policy will populate your new group, which will mirror the Passive Learning group, and you can match your new 'My Passive Group' in subrule exceptions, or elsewhere as a condition when you want to match hosts in the Passive Learning group.

Case Study - Sister Policies
While not commonly used, sister policies can be very effective in providing additional information. At a high level, conceptually a sister policy is used in conjunction with another policy, typically to provide additional information, or possibly provide additional information that we cannot gather in a single policy. One caveat to be aware of is that if you add additional sub rules to the main policy, you may need to make additional logic adjustments to the sister policy.

For this example, we will assume that we are starting with a policy similar to the template policy for Primary Classification. If utilizing the newer Forescout Professional Services policy set, under policy manager this policy may be named 'Enterprise Discover'. If using the older policy set, it may be labeled as 'Classification'. For this particular case study, we are creating a sister policy to give us a mechanism to track pending and irresolvable devices.

So before we create the sister policy let's review the high level parts of the policy that we will be pairing it with.

1.1.1 Enterprise Discover

Scope - All IPs

Main Rule Condition - No conditions

Subrules

> NAT Devices
>
> Windows
>
> VoIP
>
> Network Devices
>
> Printers
>
> Linux/Unix
>
> Macintosh
>
> Mobile
>
> Known Miscellaneous Devices
>
> Unknown Miscellaneous Devices

For each of the subrules, in our main policy we have an action of 'add to group' for that subrule with a relevant group name.

Preparing the main policy for the sister policy we will start by adding an action to the main rule of "add to group" for a new group, which we will call EnterpriseDiscoverSister.

Now we will create our sister policy.

Name: 1.1.1b Enterprise Discover Sister

Main Rule Condition: Member of group - 'EnterpriseDiscoverSister'

Subrule NAT Devices

      Condition: Member of Group - NAT Devices

Subrule Windows

      Condition: Member of Group - Windows

Subrule VoIP

      Condition: Member of Group - VoIP

Subrule Network Devices

      Condition: Member of Group - Network Devices

Subrule Printers

      Condition: Member of Group - Printers

Subrule Linux/Unix

      Condition: Member of Group - Linux/Unix

Subrule Macintosh

      Condition: Member of Group - Macintosh

Subrule Mobile

      Condition: Member of Group - Mobile

Subrule Known Miscellaneous Devices

      Condition: Member of Group - Known Miscellaneous Devices

Subrule Unknown Miscellaneous Devices

      Condition: Member of Group - Unknown Miscellaneous Devices

Subrule Pending or Irresolvable

Condition: No Conditions

Actions: ???

Notice that the conditions are just matching the groups that devices were added to in the Discover Policy. Since the Main Rule for the main 1.1.1 Enterprise Discover policy adds to our sister group, when devices match the main rule, they will then match the criteria for main rule of the sister policy. Initially, a device that is still being processed by the 1.1.1 policy won't match any of the higher subrules of 1.1.1b and will be matched by the final subrule with no conditions. Once a host has matched a subrule in the 1.1.1 policy and is added to that subrule group, it will match the higher subrule in the 1.1.1b policy. The only devices that will remain in the past subrule for an extended period of time are ones that get stuck as pending or irresolvable. By adding a scheduled action on the last subrule, you can track devices that took an extended amount of time to resolve. If a small environment you may be fine with an email notification scheduled with a 5 minute delay, which would notify you when a host didn't resolve within 5 minutes. In larger environments email may not be practical, and you may want to consider a syslog or other notification, or potentially just a permanent 'add to group' with the same 5 minute delay. If additional subrules are added to 1.1.1, you will need to add subrules to 1.1.1b. In more secure environments, the device may be added to a group for restriction or quarantine after 5 minutes, rather than just a notification sent out.

Optionally you could use as few as two subrules for the sister policy, and have the first subrule with OR conditions matching all of the various groups, rather than matching them in individual subrules. My personal preference is to have the groups as separate subrules. Another option would be to organize the groups with logical hierarchy, if the groups Windows, VoIP, Printers and so on all had a parent group of "Discovery Groups" as used in the Forescout Professional Services policy set, you could use just two subrules and have the first sub rule just match the parent "Discovery Groups" group, and anything left over for the second subrule would be devices that were in either pending or irresolvable states.

13. Switch Plugin

In this chapter we are going to take a look at some of the miscellaneous advanced settings within the switch plugin.

SNMP / SSH tuning

The Advanced settings section of the permissions tab for a switch has additional options for SNMP and SSH parameters. One change that is briefly mentioned in the switch plugin help file is to modify the timeout and retry values with -t 30 -r 3 for SNMP. In the event you have switches that are flip flopping from a status of green check to red x, adjusting these values can stabilize the reported status, resulting in a consistent status of the desired green check mark.

IP to MAC mapping

If your environment uses VRFs (Virtual Routing and Forwarding instances) on the devices acting as layer 3 gateways, you may need to check this box. By default, only the global table is checked when doing ARP reads. If VRFs are not use in your environment, there is no need to check the box "Read - IP to MAC mapping (ARP table) for VRF's".

Connectivity Groups

Rather than waiting to resolve IP to MAC information proper configuration of connectivity groups can enhance IP address resolution timing for a host. Complete configuration of connectivity groups requires properly configuring the groups under the switch plugin, and configuring a corresponding policy with the expedite discovery action. With the default interval of 10 minutes for periodic ARP queries, the time to correlate the MAC and IP address can be in excess of 10 minutes. With connectivity groups configured, that time can be reduced from minutes to seconds.

Before Connectivity groups:

Device connects

Switch reports MAC address to appliance via configured MAC notification traps or via periodic polling from appliance

At next ARP query interval, when appliance queries the layer 3 gateway device, the MAC is mapped to IP.

After connectivity groups:

Device connects

switch reports MAC address to appliance, either via configured traps for MAC notification or via periodic polling from appliance

Device matches policy with action of "Expedite IP Discovery"

Appliance directs a triggered ARP query to the corresponding layer 3 device.

How to configure:

Under the switch plugin, configure connectivity groups to logically map layer 2 and layer 3 devices.

Under the switch plugin, for only the layer 3 devices check the box "Allow IP discovery from Connectivity Group"

Under the Options, Internal network section, check the box for "Handle new hosts with a MAC address and no IPv4 address"

Under the policy tab, configure a policy with a scope of devices without an IP address and add a subrule with an action of "Expedite IP Discovery". Additional sub rules may be needed above the subrule to expedite discovery, if you have known device types where the MAC address will not be discovered.

Additionally, depending on your global setting for Network admission resolve delay, you may want to have a lower value for this specific policy.

Configuration flags

For Cisco devices, the cdm:on advanced flag allows the switch plugin to pull full device configs from the devices and you can then write policies to look for certain lines in the config, which can be used to audit the configurations of the switches themselves. There are additional configuration flags, some of which are detailed in the switch plugin help file, for specific cases such as assigning SGT tags, forwarding SNMP traps, verifying disconnected devices behind VoIP phones, and more.

VLANs

On the switch side, changing VLANs as a restriction allows you to move the device to a VLAN that has been restricted. When using the action of 'change VLAN', the VLAN can be changed by either VLAN name or VLAN number. The VLAN that you are changing to has to exist on the switch, as the Forescout appliance does not add a new VLAN, but merely changes the data VLAN on the port. So if two locations have separate naming and numbering for the VLANs, you can't make the change in a single subrule for both, and typically would need to match the location in your policy logic, and have a separate sub rule for each of the two locations. From a networking perspective, you still need to do the rest of the provisioning. The VLAN will need to be routed, and will typically need services such as DHCP.

Note: Just because your VLAN is named 'restrict' or 'quarantine', naming alone isn't enough to actually restrict the endpoints connected to that VLAN. Typically the network or security team would restrict the VLAN itself, possibly via ACLs on the network equipment such as a VLAN ACL. When using 802.1x, the VLAN action is slightly different, as it typically uses the action of "RADIUS Authorize" to perform a CoA, rather than the 'Assign to VLAN' action.

In many cases, the VLAN change can be done by either SNMP or CLI, and is typically faster than writing an ACL to a switch.

Port flap

If there is a port with multiple hosts on the data VLAN, all will be affected by the VLAN change. Further, the default mechanism is to flap the port when changing the VLAN, so that then endpoint goes link down, and will know to re-request DHCP. If the device has a static IP address configured, it may end up isolated and not be able to send traffic, as the static IP address would not be on the new VLAN.

If there is a phone connected to the port with a computer connected to the phone, and the phone is powered by PoE, the phone will power cycle. This may not be the desired behavior as it will drop a phone call in progress. Sometimes the phone call is more important than changing the data VLAN. If the phone does not use PoE and instead is powered via a different mechanism, then the endpoint behind the phone may not be aware that there was a VLAN change, as the link will not flap if the phone doesn't lose power.

If SecureConnector is on the device behind the phone, it is possible to change the VLAN without flapping the port, using the checkbox "Do not bounce switch ports for hosts with SecureConnector".

When dealing with VLAN changes, in general you want to make sure that your policies cover both the range where you are moving from as well as the VLANs that you are moving to.

ACLs

There are two similar options.

Access Port ACL

Using the Access Port ACL action, you need to specify the actual syntax for the ACL lines to use. Make sure to test on a switch, as misconfigured syntax is the most common error seen with these which will cause them to not apply correctly.

Additionally, with the Access Port ACL, you have the option to select an ACL from the ACL repository. The ACL repository lets you have a single location within the switch plugin rather than specifying ACL lines in each individual ACL policy action

The Access port ACL action does also require the configuration of the Switch Options configuration flag of all:acl_action_type:access_port_acl

Endpoint Address ACL

In this case, you just state what to allow or block, and Forescout dynamically creates the ACL for you.

For both methods, there is the option to choose IP or MAC ACLs. In prior versions of Cisco switches, the MAC ACLs operated differently and blocked protocols like ARP, which effectively limited most communication. In newer versions, with a MAC ACL applied, ARP, IPv4 and IPv6 are typically allowed regardless of what the ACL states, due to how these protocols are handled within the switch. While a MAC ACL can block other layer 2 protocols, those are not common in most environments.

ACLs on the switch are different than ACLs on wireless. On the wireless side, you can reference a pre-existing ACL on the controller, rather than sending ACL lines individually as is done with the switch plugin.

If using multiple different ACLs on the switch, you may need to be cautious about ACL length, so that you don't exceed the switch platform's TCAM table.

Switch Plugin

14. DNS Enforce Plugin

In this chapter we will give a brief overview of the DNS Enforce Plugin.

The DNS Enforce Plugin allows an alternate mechanism to enabling some of the HTTP actions within Forescout in cases where you may not be able to see HTTP requests in the monitored (channel) traffic. Functionally, it uses a DNS redirection rather than redirecting based on the HTTP GET request. On the Forescout side, configuration of the DNS Enforce at a minimum requires configuring an additional address in the Module for the management interface of an appliance. On the network side, configure the DHCP server for the network to hand out the new address configured as the primary DNS for the subnet.

Subsequently, when an endpoint makes a DNS request, if the appliance has an action pending to apply to the host, it will reply with the IP address of the appliance. In the event the appliance doesn't have a pending action for the host, it can be configured to either just not reply to the DNS query, and let the host query the secondary DNS server. In order to configure to not reply, make sure the checkbox "Enable DNS resolution forwarding for unrestricted hosts" is deselected, under the DNS Enforce configuration page.

There are some tradeoffs here though. You don't want your Forescout appliance proxying all the DNS for your environment. Typically only enable forwarding

15. External Classifier Plugin

In this chapter, we will be taking a brief look at the External Classifier Plugin.

The External Classifier plugin allows you to query an external source for a set of MAC addresses, however it has some limitations. Each appliance is able to do a single query for each FTP and LDAP to query information. This may sound very similar to some of the functionality available with the DEX module, however unlike DEX, the external classifier is included as part of the Core Extensions module, and does not require additional licensing. So if the basic functionality is sufficient, then the external classifier module may be sufficient for a basic task.

One sample use case would be a list of MAC address exceptions stored on an FTP server. Perhaps you have a group that you don't want to have permissions to directly change in Forescout, but you want them to be able to add exceptions. They can add the exceptions to the FTP file, and then Forescout will periodically query the FTP file based on the interval configured in the external classifier, and the endpoints could then be matched by the external classifier property.

Another use case would be to query LDAP for a list of printer MAC addresses, to use as identifying them as known corporate assets.

As mentioned earlier, each appliance can do ONE of each FTP and LDAP, so if you have 2 separate FTP queries, you would need to configure 2 separate appliances, but one appliance could do one FTP and one LDAP query. For more robust functionality, DEX would be another option.

16. Advanced Tools Plugin

In this chapter, we will be covering the additional functionalities enabled with the Advanced Tools Plugin

Previously the Advanced Tools plugin was a separate plugin that needed to be downloaded and installed separately. With the grouping of plugins into Modules, it is now included in the Core Extensions module.

Additional Properties

The Advanced Tools plugin adds the following property items, which will be discussed individually:

Windows Manageable SecureConnector (via any interface)

Labels

Counters

Segment Path

Run Script on CounterACT

Add Value to List

Note: In order to use these items, the advanced tools plugin needs to be running on your managing appliances.

Windows Manageable SecureConnector (via any interface)

Under the Options Menu, there is a single checkbox listed under the Advanced Tools item to enable this feature. While the help file warns that enabling this feature may cause significant processor and memory resources on the appliance, I personally have not seen any noticeable impact to system resources with this feature enabled, however as a cautionary measure, the recommendation is still to not check the box unless you need this feature.

The use case for this feature requires that you are both using SecureConnector in the environment AND that you have hosts that will be dual-homed. Without the feature enabled, the endpoint will be seen as managed on the SecureConnector connected interface and unmanaged on the other interface. Depending on how your policies are configured, the device being seen as unmanaged may result in it being unnecessarily marked as "non compliant" or marked for restriction or quarantine, or possibly generating unnecessary log messages or administrative emails.

With this feature enabled, the second interface can match the property even though that interface is not where the SecureConnector connection is originating. This can be used to match in a separate subrule, so that these addresses are not marked as unmanageable or noncompliant.

Labels

Labels can be used as an additional property and can be added as a policy ACTION or can be checked as a policy CONDITION.

While they may initially appear to have very similar functionality as groups and lists, labels have some additional functionality, specifically that we have the additional action available of "delete label", where we don't have that as an available option for groups or lists, as "remove from group" or "remove from list" are not available actions.

Counters

Counters add the option to use and clear a numeric counter. Setting or incrementing a counter is done by a policy ACTION, where the counter value would be checked as a policy CONDITION.

A few sample use cases for counters would be repeatedly matching a policy, flexible matching (3 out of 5), or weighted scoring.

Repeat Matches

Maybe you have a policy to catch offenders for unwanted software such as peer to peer. Util

Grouping Matches

More flexible than basic boolean conditions in some cases (At least 3 out of 5)

Say you have five compliance policies, and you want to see which devices are compliant for at least three out of the five.

Using a counter action on the individual policies with a common counter name can be used, with each of the five individual policies incrementing the counter by one, and then on a separate policy, can just check which devices have a that counter with a value of 3 or more. This can be much easier than performing the same task using boolean and/or logic for the same task.

Weighted scoring

Perhaps when it comes to compliance you have certain things that you consider more critical than others. Similar to the previous example, different compliance policies can have different increment values for the same counter.

AV not running - increment 50

External USB Device Attached - increment 30

Drive not Encrypted - increment 20

Running P2P software - increment 20

Using the same counter, you can write an additional policy to look at the counter value, and perform different actions based on the overall total. Maybe if the counter is over 80 you have more aggressive actions than if the counter is under 40.

Segment Path

Depending on the amount of hierarchy in your configured Segment design the segment path may have additional information which can be useful.

The segment path property lists out the hierarchy of your specific segment in Segment Manager. Here is a sample name/path pairing:

Segment name: NYC_Data_VLAN

Segment Path: /Segments/In Scope/Northeast Region/New York/NY_Appliance1/NYC/NYC_Data_VLAN

Notice that the segment name is included at the end of the segment path, and the segment path also lists the higher branches in the hierarchy. So, if you wanted to match based on the region, rather than having to match all the individual segment names you could use the criteria "Segment Path CONTAINS Northeast Region".

Run Script on CounterACT

Rather than running a script on the endpoint, there may be cases where you want to run a query about an endpoint on the managing appliance.

One early use for the "Run Script on CounterACT" would be to run the Linux curl command to retrieve the webpage from an endpoint and parse the output.

The "Run Script on CounterACT" functionality also acts as the framework for the following device properties:

URL content

Managing appliance will connect on the specified web port and parses the resulting output received back.

snmpwalk output

Managing appliance will connect to the endpoint via SNMP and parse output based on what is configured in the property condition

SSH command output

The managing appliance for an endpoint will connect via SSH and attempt to run an SSH command and parse output based on what is configured in the property configuration.

Add Value to List

This one is pretty self-explanatory, add value to list allows you to dynamically add items to a Forescout list by policy. One downside is that you need to explicitly type the list name, as it does not include a drop down selector.

17. DEX/Connect Module

In this chapter, we will be providing a high level overview of the DEX/Connect module.

Background

The exeExtend Connect module is one of the most flexible modules in the Forescout platform. In the past, various names have been given to parts of the functionality it provides, so you may have heard of it referred to by one or more of the following names:

Open Integration Module (OIM)

ControlFabric

Data Exchange (DEX)

Connect

Web API

Note: As this is an extended module, there is some additional licensing cost associated with it. The cost can seem high if you are only using it for a single purpose. If you have multiple different use cases for it, then it can provide additional value for your Forescout investment. Extended modules can be tested with a complimentary 90 day demo license. If you wish to take the trial license option, I would recommend waiting until you are at the point that you are ready to test before you install, as the timer starts when you install the module.

At a high level the functionality provided by this is to integrate with a variety of other platform types, via Web API calls, SQL, and other mechanisms.

This provides an extensible framework for data sharing with systems where there is not an existing Forescout module or extended module.

Components

The three primary components are as follows:

Web API - Query Forescout from an external server/platform

Data Exchange - Query external servers/platforms or receive from external servers/platforms

Connect - Write your own integration (or use one someone else has written)

DEX

Data Exchange can operate in push and pull modes and act as both client and server. Common protocols used include SQL, LDAP and Web based (REST API)

The difference between client and server is who makes the initial request. The difference between push and pull is which direction is the data passed.

As a client, pull means Forescout is requesting data and receiving a response back.

As a client, push means Forescout is pushing data to an external platform.

As a server, pull means that an external source requested data and Forescout replied with data (handled by Web API)

As a server, push means that an external source pushed data to Forescout.

Configuration of DEX

When dealing with data coming in from an external source, you will also define the remote platforms by either IP, DNS Name, or URL, depending on the connection method being used. Additionally, you will typically define one or more properties. Depending on what type of data you are receiving, these can be a single property, a list of values, a composite property where one query maps out multiple individual properties, or just the record existing. Data types can be integer, string, boolean, IP address, MAC address, or date. Be careful when configuring properties. If you make a mistake you may need to delete the property and start over, as some items cannot be edited.

Connect

Connect allows for writing of apps to integrate with the Forescout platform. At a high level, it provides a streamlined mechanism to write your own integration or to leverage one of the community contributed apps.

Apps can be found at the following location:

Https://github.com/Forescout/eyeExtend-Connect

Note: These apps are community contributed and not supported by Forescout Customer Support.

The App building guide is linked on the github page and gives steps about creating the various files, including system.conf, property.conf, optional policy templates as well as sample scripts.

Web API

The Web API enables third party device to retrieve Forescout properties via a web interface, with JSON results returned.

Within the Options menu, define a user and optionally restrict to queries from just specific address ranges.

Here are some samples:

Query hosts that match a specific policy subruld:

https://{EM.IP]/api/hosts?matchRuleId

Based on endpoint IP address:

https://{EM.IP}/api/hosts/ip/ {ipv4}

https://{EM.IP}/api/hosts/ip/ {ipv4} ?fields= {prop},..,{prop_n}

Based on endpoint MAC address:

https://{EM.IP}/api/hosts/mac/ {mac}

https://{EM.IP}/api/hosts/mac/ {mac} ?fields= {prop},..,{prop_n}

Based on the web service object ID of the full endpoint listing; the object ID is specified in the self link that is returned for each endpoint.

https://{EM.IP}/api/hosts/ {obj_ID}

https://{EM.IP}/api/hosts/ {obj_ID} ?fields= {prop},..,{prop_n}

18. Reports

In this chapter we will be taking a brief overview of the reports portal.

Launching the Portal

The reports portal can be launched a few different ways. You can use Ctrl-R from the main GUI, select report from the Reports menu at the top, or select reports from the ... tab on the top right. The portal can also be accessed at https://x.x.x.x/report in a browser. If there is an EM in the environment, you will want to launch the reports portal using the address of the EM, not an individual appliance.

Creating a Report

Reports are made by selecting a template type to start with. Policy Details is one of the most common templates.

Name

Reports need a unique name. Common format is to name the policy based on which policy the report is for, as the default of "policy Details" isn't very descriptive.

Reports Scope

You can run a report against all IPs or against a selection of Segments that you have defined.

For a template such as policy details, select which particular policy you want to run the report again.

Next to the dropdown for policy is the button 'Edit policy labels'. The 'Edit policy labels' option will allow you to select which subrules you want to include in the report. For example, if you were building a report on your Antivirus policy, you may not care about the 95% of your devices that are up to date, so you could deselect those subrules. Additionally, you can select various RGB values for the subrules for graphs (if desired).

Display

The next section after scope is display. This section allows you to select which columns you want in your report. In most cases, some of the columns may not be of much use, so you may want to remove some of them and possibly add others.

In order to change the columns, click the edit button.

You can select one column to sort by, and can select either ascending or descending. For a report like Antivirus updates, you might want to add the column for AV update date. Note, there is a column for 'last update time' which is not the same thing. The column for AV update is 'Windows Antivirus Update Date :Value : All items'

Although they are listed in a vertical list, they will be columns in the report, so up and down actually refer to left and right in the column order.

If you click the edit button to expand the column list, you will need to select either OK or Cancel in the table column sections or it won't let you run or save the report, as those buttons will appear grayed out.

If you are running a report against a large number of devices, it is strongly recommended to remove unnecessary columns. I have seen report emails fail because the report was so large that it exceeded the organizations mail attachment size limit.

You have the option to select PDF or CSV format for your report. CSV won't include graphs.

Schedule

Finally you have the option to schedule. You can just save the report without running, or you can schedule a recurrence and an email address of where to send. Scheduling options are somewhat limited, as you can choose daily or weekly at a specified time in half hour intervals.

One thing to keep in mind with scheduling. If you run the report after hours, such as 2AM, then the hosts may not be online, and as a result may not match the policy, and therefore would not be displayed in the report.

19. Virtual Firewall

In this chapter, we will be taking a brief overview of the functionality of the virtual firewall.

The virtual firewall allows you to block access to or from an endpoint. You can configure blocking rules and blocking exceptions for either traffic to an endpoint or traffic from an endpoint.

If there is a virtual firewall applied to a host, the blocking rules and exceptions, in conjunction with the global virtual firewall exceptions will determine what traffic is blocked.

Globally the system will generate exceptions based on your system configuration. For example, it will still allow you to connect to the appliance for things like HTTP login for Guest Registration, or allowing SecureConnector traffic to the appliance. In addition, authentication servers configured under Options are allowed.

Traffic monitoring

Virtual Firewall is only effective for traffic that the Packet Engine can see. If you are capturing traffic at the distribution layer, and you have a pair of distribution switches where the traffic could go through either switch, make sure that you are capturing traffic from both switches.

Traffic Injection

For traffic that matches a blocking rule but not one of the exceptions, the virtual firewall will inject a TCP reset if a TCP SYN packet is seen, and a ICMP unreachable if a UDP packet is seen. The traffic injection must be allowed on the network device where the response interface is connected. Some network features such as uRPF (Unicast Reverse Path Forwarding) checks can block this injected traffic.

When to Use

Virtual firewall can be used in places where you don't have managed switches or in places where switchport restrictions may not be practical. For example, if you have a VPN terminating security appliance, with hundreds or thousands of VPN clients connected, shutting down the port where the VPN device is connected, or applying an ACL or changing the VLAN would potentially affect thousands of clients. However, if you are seeing the traffic in your channel, you can inject selective blocking on a per host basis, if only some of the VPN clients are matching the virtual firewall action. Additionally, virtual firewall can be used as a backup method in conjunction with another action. For example, some organizations use a combination of switchport ACL AND Virtual Firewall, so that if the ACL does not apply for any reason, that there is still some restriction taken against the endpoint.

20. **Threat Protection**

In this chapter we will be taking a look at the threat protection functionality. Threat protection is covered extensively in the Administrator guide, so we will focus here on a brief overview.

Threat protection prerequisites

- Environment set to Full Enforcement Mode
- Channels properly configured and receiving traffic
- Valid eyeControl license (if using Flexx licensing)
- Threat protection enabled under Options-Threat protection
- Active Response Range configured
- Response portion of the channel needs to be able to inject spoofed traffic into the network.

For now, we will assume all those prerequisites have been met.

How it Works

Threat Protection listens for questionable traffic behavior directed toward hosts contained within the Active Response

217

Range. Some of the initial behavior that it is monitoring for are various scan categories, such as Finger, HTTP, Login, NetBIOS, SNMP, ping sweeps, and UDP/TCP port scans.

By default if a three probes are seen within the specified period (5 probes for port scans), it is then monitored for the monitor period (12 hours by default). If no further items are seen within that time period, the item is removed from the threats list. So if you see an item in the threats tab with a timer value of 11:30 for the column 'expires in', then it saw a recent event. If the value in the column was 2:01 then it has not seen any additional probes in almost 10 hours. If there is an additional probe, the timer is reset.

Vertical Scan - checking the same host on multiple ports, for example scanning TCP ports 21, 23, 25, 80, 443 on a single host.

Horizontal Scan - checking the same PORT on multiple hosts, for example scanning 5 different hosts on TCP port 80.

If you have legitimate devices that are permitted to scan your network, such as an SNMP monitoring server that would be potentially scanning SNMP, then you can add those exceptions. You can allow anything for a legitimate device, or could restrict to exempting a specific port, and if scans were seen on other ports they would still trigger as a threat.

Perhaps you have a known vulnerability scanner in your environment such as Tenable or Rapid7. If so, you might exclude ANY activity for that scanner IP from triggering as a threat.

If you are enabling threat protection for Email worms, you will want to enter your legitimate email servers, so that they aren't seen as malicious.

Monitor Mode

Monitor mode will detect threats. The appliance will send out fake traffic, called marks. So if a host was scanning across the network and a malicious device sent out probe to .1, .2, .3, and .4, Forescout may respond to some, such as .2 and .4, masquerading as a legitimate host. If the suspect endpoint then subsequently attempts to connect to .2 or .4 on that port, Forescout knows that there is no legitimate reason for that connection, as it knows that is not a real resource that the connection is attempting to connect to. When the suspect endpoint tries to connect, that is considered a 'bite' event.

Blocking Mode

Blocking mode will take further action against the host. We have two separate options, port block and host block. For port block, it is specific to the port, such as TCP/80. For host block, it is any traffic from that host. So if a host was scanning on port 80, if the thresholds were exceeded and port block was enabled as the action, it would send out TCP resets for any TCP SYN packet seen on port 80 for the host. In the host block mode, it would send out TCP resets for any TCP SYN packet seen, regardless of port. Under Block Method, there is an option to escalate from port block to host block. So if a host had multiple port block actions, it would escalate to a host block against that host IP.

In addition to legitimate traffic exceptions, you can also manually set state for a device to ignore, monitor, port block or host block.

21. Architectural Overview and Considerations

This chapter covers a mix of high level concepts, questions that you should be able to answer about your desired deployment, and various points to consider.

Let's start with the assumption that you have not yet purchased the Forescout equipment for your environment.

Here are some of the high level questions to start with:

How many appliances do you need?

ActiveCare Basic, Advanced, or Premium?

What additional licenses are needed?

How many endpoints are you licensing?

Is failover/recovery needed?

What architecture type - Centralized, Distributed, or hybrid?

Is this a new implementation or an expansion of an existing implementation?

Is there a preference between physical or virtual for EM and appliances?

Is SPAN / tap traffic part of the implementation?

Implementation type - visibility only? or control as well?

Enterprise Manager and Appliances

The two device types in a Forescout deployment are the Enterprise Manager (EM) and the Appliances.

If you only have one appliance, there is no need to have an Enterprise Manager, as you can just configure everything on the single appliance.

If you are migrating from an environment with one appliance, you can import the settings for that appliance to the Enterprise Manager and then add additional appliances without having to configure from scratch.

In most environments, there will be more than one appliance, so the Enterprise Manager acts as a single point of configuration. After the EM is initialized, the individual appliances are added and then assigned address ranges to manage, in addition to other infrastructure such as switches and wireless. The physical hardware used is the same for physical appliances and EM, but the sizing is different. Sizing for an EM is up to 200 appliances that it can manage, whereas sizing for an appliances is up to 20,000 endpoints. The EM manages appliances, the appliances manage endpoints. Configuration changes made then get pushed to the individual appliances. The EM maintains a management connection out to the appliances. Software updates to modules will be pushed out to appliances from the EM. In the event an appliance is offline when an update to a module happens, that particular appliance would receive the update the next time it connected. If an appliance loses connectivity to the EM, it will still operate with the policy and configuration that it has. The EM would not display the resulting policy counts for the appliance while it is disconnected.

One common misconception is that the EM has some "master database" that includes all the endpoints and information in the environment. This is not the case. When you view information in the EM, the EM is querying the appliances and receiving results as you click on various items in the GUI.

The 5100 series

At the time of this writing, the 5100 Series is the current series of appliance, and the older CT series appliances are not being sold. The legacy CT series appliances utilized per-appliance licensing (PAL), where the new 5100 series uses Flexx licensing. With the older PAL licensing, a CT-4000 included both the hardware and the endpoint licenses for 4000 devices.

To accommodate a variety of preferences, licensing under the newer model can be either permanent or term-based, and appliance licensing can be scaled up on a "pay as you grow" model. So you could select a hardware appliance that can support up to 20,000 endpoints, but could start with a smaller group of endpoint licenses, such as 1000 or 5000, and then add additional licenses as you expand your deployment.

License Count

Most enterprises have no idea of their true endpoint count before installing Forescout. Typical rough estimates are 4-5 times the number of users, but in some environments that may be a low estimate. Forescout is licensed by IP address, so if an endpoint has two IP addresses within the internal network range, it will take up two licenses towards the license count. Also, devices that have gone offline still count towards your license totals. Typically there is consideration for future growth as well. If licenses are being handled as a one time purchase up front, typically growth anticipation is included in the calculations, in some cases planning guidelines can be 10-30% per year for expected endpoint increase. Additionally, devices that go offline are still counted towards the total, so your purge timer may also have implications on whether you might exceed your expected license count.

Deployment types- centralized, decentralized, hybrid

Centralized typically has all appliances at one location or a select few locations (such as in the enterprise datacenters).

Decentralized has appliances at each location.

Hybrid has some sites with their own appliances, and some sites either handled by a regional aggregate appliance group, or by a centralized appliance in the datacenter.

Depending on the total count of sites, a decentralized deployment with hundreds of sites may take years, depending on the logistics of physically getting the appliances to the various locations. A centralized deployment can be set up in as little as a day if there is a low count of appliances.

If using network taps for SPAN traffic, a decentralized deployment will give more visibility of traffic at the individual sites, where a centralized deployment would only have visibility to SPAN traffic that traversed the datacenter.

Dual environments

Some organizations have two or more independent Forescout environments. These may each have their own EM, or some could be standalone environments with just a single appliance.

Networks of differing sensitivity levels, such as separate networks that are airgapped and physically discontiguous

Isolated networks for alternate environments, such as dedicated development and test networks

Large environments which exceed the 200 appliance limit, can have more than 200 appliances by logically splitting the environment into two or more separate groups, each with less than 200 appliances, which then are independent of each other.

Isolated networks for things like guest access, in which some customers have completely separate physical infrastructure for guest, including separate physical access points, controllers, and internet connections, or similar cases with multiple airgapped independent networks.

SPAN / Tap traffic

Used for Threat detection (built in functionality to check for potentially malicious traffic)

Used to gather information about host traffic flows

Some protocols are parsed further for additional information gathering (HTTP user Agent strings, DHCP requests/replies, etc)

Additionally, traffic response can be used for HTTP redirects, HTTP login for guest registration, HTTP notifications, and the Virtual Firewall action to restrict endpoints without using ACLs or changing VLANs.

If Layer 2 traffic (learned from same broadcast domain as the endpoint), also used for ARP learning.

License types

Let's take a look at the individual licenses

eyeSight - license enables visibility across the enterprise

eyeManage - license for the Enterprise Manager(s), included by default with Flexx (previously an add on under the older licensing model)

eyeSegment - used for

eyeControl - license for restricting hosts via control actions

eyeRecover - license for failover and resiliency for appliances eyeExtend - License for various extended modules, for orchestration functionality

eyeSight is the base license for visibility, and with Flexx licensing eyeManage is also included. If not using virtual managers, you will still need the hardware for the manager(s), even though the licensing is included.

eyeControl is the license for restricting hosts via control actions

If you are just using Forescout for visibility, this license is not necessary.

eyeExtend licensing covers extended modules, such as Splunk, DEX, and others.

Which modules do you need? Splunk? DEX? Connect? If you aren't sure, you may want to review what modules are available and compare against what products are in use in your organization in a discussion with your Forescout contact or Forescout partner. This functionality can bring in additional properties from external sources, or in some cases enable additional automation flows, such as a SIEM platform correlating an event and then sending a message to Forescout in order to facilitate a device restriction as a result of the correlation, utilizing Forescout as the enforcement mechanism.

eyeRecover is the license for appliance failover and resiliency

On the appliance side, we have different options for appliance resiliency. One option is the use of HA pairs, and another option is the usage of Failover Clustering. For HA, two appliances act as a logical pair, each device has it's own node IP address, and there is a shared virtual address where the active device in the pair will respond to. IP addresses to manage are assigned to the logical pair, and the active device in the HA pair would manage the endpoints. In the case that the active device failed, the second device in the pair would take over and take responsibility for managing the endpoints. The primary node uses block replication to synchronize information to the secondary node. HA switchover is not preemptive. If the original device recovered after the failure, it does not retake control, and instead just acts as the secondary node. Due to the low latency requirements for the block replication, the two devices in an HA pair are typically quite close from a distance perspective. While they could be in neighboring buildings, the two nodes in a pair are commonly in the same room.

Failover clustering allows you to have more of an active/active grouping. You could have 4 appliances underprovisioned at 70%, and if one of the devices failed, the other 3 could take over and handle the endpoints. Or you could have a nearby location with extra capacity that can take over in the event of a failure. You could have two sites each provisioned at 50% of appliance capacity, and if one failed, the other device could take over.

A Focal appliance is the term for a device being used to connect off to a third party platform/server for part of an integration. Say for example you have a MDM integration as

229

part of your configuration with a specific appliance configured to connect off to the MDM platform and retrieve properties.

When dealing with focal appliances, the preferred method is to use HA pairs. If the primary fails and the secondary takes over, it will still use the assigned virtual address to connect to this third party platform.

When dealing with channel traffic analysis via traffic from network taps/SPAN, it is also recommended to use HA pairs. Having two nodes in an HA pair that are both receiving traffic, only the active node will be actively processing the traffic with the packet engine.

One other key differentiator that can influence which of the two methods you may want to use is that with an HA pair, the decision to switchover is made by the secondary node, whereas in failover clustering the decision is made by the EM, and then communicated to the appliances. In the event that there are communication issues between the EM and the appliances, it could have adverse effects on the switchover.

If Forescout is just being used for visibility, resiliency may not be as important.

eyeManage - license covering the EM, included with Flexx

On the EM side, there are also options available for resiliency. Similar to appliances, one option is to use HA pairs, where two act as a single logical node. For the EM, there is a secondary option called a 'Recovery Manager', where a device has the configuration information replicated to it. This is not a full block replication, so the recovery manager can be located at an entirely different physical location. For some customers with an international presence, the Recovery Manager may not even be on the same continent. These can also be combined. So, you could have an HA pair in one location, and a Recovery HA pair at a second location. EM resiliency is included in the eyeManage license, but if using physical devices you will still need to procure those devices.

Virtual devices

VMware, Hyper-V and KVM are supported hypervisors, as well as cloud based (cloud based are recommended for managing cloud based endpoints and are out of scope for this book)

In most cases, it is more common to use virtual devices for EM. You can mix and match in the environment, you could have some appliances physical, and some virtual.

Virtual appliances present additional complexity if forwarding SPAN traffic to appliances, due to extra logistics and logical overhead to get the replicated traffic to the VM for the packet engine to process.

Forescout VM recommendations are to have dedicated resources with hard allocations for disk, memory, and CPU. The sizing guide online can give the current values, as the minimum values for CPU and memory may increase in newer versions.

In some cases the decision for physical vs virtual is based on the location for the appliance. For example, if it is a remote location, or a location where there may be significant delays such as customs delays getting a physical device into a country, a virtual device may be an easier choice. Another consideration can be the robustness of the VM environment. In some cases, a new VM can be provisioned in a matter of minutes, where in other environments, the provisioning process may take weeks due to administrative hurdles.

Cross Functional Teams

In many cases, it is either the network or security group that is responsible for getting Forescout into the organization. Ideally, both groups are working together utilizing the Forescout platform. Many groups can benefit from the information, the customers with multiple groups able to access the GUI and view information recognize better overall value and return on investment (ROI) from the implementation. The most successful implementations typically have support from multiple groups. Some of the groups that can be included in an implementation can be the obvious ones like network, security, operations, help desk. Other less common ones that may be involved could be HR (for repeat offenders resulting in disciplinary action), legal (for specific terms and conditions and other phrasing), and even lobby/building administrative assistants or others that would be responsible for granting guest access.

Use Cases:
Visibility Only
(no restrictions)

Some use Forescout purely for visibility. In some cases, this is all they are looking to achieve, where in other cases, the long term objective is control, but they want to evaluate the current state of the environment before deciding what path they want to take for control.

Some customers initially implement Forescout as a secondary check in order to validate other existing platforms that were performing certain checks. In many cases, the visibility provided by the Forescout platform can be useful to a variety of different groups in the organization.

Guest Access
Guest access can be via HTTP login action, or via an 802.1x redirect in the case of wireless. Via an HTTP login action is common, however typically it is also coupled with a change of VLAN to restrict what access the user is granted, both before and after authentication. In some cases devices are identified as guest and then restricted until authenticated, and then allowed certain traffic outbound (but typically not allowed to access internal organization resources).

Preconnect

evaluation (assume bad, allow if good)

In a pre-connect environment, devices start in a restricted state, typically either via a default ACL on the switchport, or starting in a 'lobby VLAN' with minimal network access. From there, the device is evaluated by Forescout, and if found to be trusted, it is either moved to the production VLAN, or the default ACL removed, and the endpoint has full access as a result

Postconnect

(assume good, restrict if bad)

In a post connect configuration, device initially is unrestricted, however if it is found to be malicious or noncompliant, it may receive restricted access or be kicked off of the network.

802.1x

While many customers use Forescout as an alternative to 802.1x, the Forescout platform is capable of authenticating endpoints via 802.1x. It can be configured in either proxy mode, where the Forescout platform proxies through to a back end RADIUS server, or it can be the authenticator, and can check devices against its own MAC Address Repository and/or check credentials against Active Directory or other servers. It can also change authorizations via a reauthentication or a change of authorization, if a policy match dictates that a device should have reduced access or no access. A complete discussion of all the moving parts for 802.1x is outside the scope of this book, although it will be touched on in a few different areas. One other possibility that some customers have chosen to implement includes differing access depending on whether it was an 802.1x login by machine certificate or by user information, or in some cases, different VLANs for specific groups based on the authenticated user's Active Directory group memberships.

Pre/post hybrid

In a pre/post hybrid setup, there may be some checks done initially, and then additional checks done later. One example would be a certificate based or other 802.1x authentication with a validated certificate chain to allow access, with additional checks performed afterwards, and restrictions or blocking if the additional checks fail.

Sample Scope Questions

What is the scope of the implementation?

Is it just visibility?

Is it just for guest access?

Wired or wireless or both?

Is it for restriction or control? If so, which one(s)? ACL, VLAN change, administrative blocking via shutting down switchports or blocking from wireless?

Is the scope user areas or datacenter or both?

Will there be separate levels of restriction? Remediation vs quarantine vs blocking?

From a compliance perspective, are the compliance requirements the same for different device types?

Are compliance requirements for datacenter the same as for user networks?

Are compliance requirements different for laptops vs desktops?

Are there compliance requirements for visiting vendors/contractors?

External Considerations

Do you have a storage location for backups? What is your expected logging level, and does your logging platform require additional licensing to accomodate?

Do you have the network switch capacity to accomodate the physical ports to connect any physical EM and appliances? In some cases, there may need to be an additional line card installed on a network switch.

What optics are needed, if any? Multimode, single mode, etc.

Are you planning using a third party platform to monitor SNMP on the appliances and EM?

For datacenter EM/appliances is there adequate cooling and power budget? Are alternate power cord connector types needed, such as twist-lock connectors?

If SPAN/tap will be used for traffic will it be coming directly from the network switch, or via a third party appliance such as a Gigamon or Ixia?

Segments

A segment is a range of one or more addresses. It has a name assignment and optionally a description.

Segments can have multiple ranges. Ranges can be specified with a starting and ending address, or by CIDR notation. Segments can be a single address or a large range. Segments don't have to follow binary bit boundaries, you could define a segment range of 10.1.1.3 to 10.1.1.37 and that would be a valid range.

In a smaller environment, you may list out each individual /24 network as an individual segment. In a large enterprise with thousands of networks that may not be practical. In larger environments, being granular down to the site level is sufficient. In some cases, customers still want to be granular and detail out specific networks at a site, such as data versus voice networks. It could also be for specific segments like PCIDSS where you may have different policies for regulatory reasons.

Segment Hierarchy

If you just have one appliance, you could just have one segment and include all your various ranges in that one named segment. In larger environments with multiple appliances, you will need additional segments in order to be able to assign different segments to different appliances to manage. For any addresses that are in your internal network but not assigned to an appliance, they are considered 'unassigned' and are typically not processed against policy.

Note: You can check for unassigned hosts on the Home tab by selecting All hosts on the upper left, and the checkbox 'Show unassigned' on the upper right.

Except for the special use case of reuse domains, as a general rule the same address range cannot be assigned to multiple appliances to manage.

As a general rule, it is recommended that you assign a segment to appliances that contains subsegments, rather than assigning a large number of individual segments in the appliance IP assignment

In Scope

    Region 1

        Site A

        Site B

        Site C

        Site D

    Region 2

        Site E

        Site F

        Site G

        Site H

In the above sample, if one appliance was covering Sites A to D, you could just assign that appliance the segment assignment of "Region 1" rather than assigning the individual sites one at a time.

Additional High level segment design questions

- How much granularity do you really need?
- Are there some hosts that you just want to run inventory and discovery on?
- Are there specific areas that need to be split up due to different policies?

Recommended Segment Manager Practices

- Utilize a high level broad range for your internal network that covers all address space, including unallocated space
- Only break out segments to the granularity level that you need
- Regularly review the "unassigned devices" to see if additional segments need to be defined or allocated to specific appliances

Starting in version 8.4 there are also additional API options for managing segments.

Group Hierarchy

Just like Segments and Policies, leading practices recommend a structured layout for groups.

Don't go crazy with groups. Some people will add groups for every single policy for every single subrule. The general guideline would be to only use an 'add to group' action if you plan to do something with that group later. There may be cases like sister policies (discussed later) where you want to add to a group for each subrule, but that is not always the case.

If you are using the Forescout Professional services policy set, then you will have the baseline groups imported before your policies.

In general, it is recommended to have a hierarchical group design, with structured parent groups.

Warning: When dealing with a group hierarchy, you do need to be careful as the Group Manager will allow drag and drop, and if you aren't careful, you could accidentally drag a group where it doesn't belong. For example, if you accidentally dragged your VoIP devices into your 'Managed Windows Devices' group, then your appliances might then start trying to evaluate your phones and other VoIP devices against your various Windows compliance policies.

Some choose group by the relevant individual policy families. Some group by major categories, so a parent group for Discovery, for example, that includes the groups used in your discovery policies.

Architectural Overview and Considerations

22. Advanced Troubleshooting

This chapter will take a look at some additional troubleshooting commands, tips, and recommendations.

In the introductory troubleshooting chapter, we covered the overview of information gathering, the basics of debugs and logs and opening a ticket. In this chapter, we will build on that foundation, and presume that you are after additional tips that may give you additional directions to look in, as well as some more reminders of the importance of the 'big picture'. Additionally, we will be looking at some miscellaneous commands that may be useful. Additionally, we will cover some additional general command line items.

Note: As a general warning, some of these commands should only be run at the explicit direction of Forescout support.

Linux Commands

While a linux background is not required, it can help to have a basic understanding of some of the command line utilities, as well as options for parsing output. Here are some common items:

ls

Similar to the Windows 'dir' command, ls will list directory contents. 'ls -al' is common as it includes file size and permissions.

ps

PS will list processes for windows. I typically use 'ps aux', listing processes and users.

top

Top will list processes with an automatic refresh, and can be sorted by processor, memory, time, or other items

hdparm

Hdparm gives information on disk, such as read speed. 'hdparm -t /dev/sda1' as an example checks read speed. Be careful to not use '-T', as that times cache reads, which will give a much higher value. Its recommended to run 2-3 times in a row, with little or no other processes running at the same time. For a Forescout device, it would be recommended to run with the Forescout services stopped. In the event there are underlying disk issues, such as a failed or failing disk, this can be used to diagnose. Under normal circumstances, disk reads should be above 200MB/sec. If there is a disk issue, they will typically be significantly lower. In the past when I have seen devices with disk issues, the read speeds have been under 50MB/sec, and under 10MB/sec in the worst cases. Typically you would also see DB_writer queue delay in the today log as a secondary indicator of a problem.

vi/vim/nano

Any of these can be used for editing. vi and vim are modal, so you switch between edit and command modes, and nano just has a single mode. My personal preference is nano, but any of the three can be used in the event that you need to edit a file.

touch

This command can be used to create a file.

cat/more/less

For the purposes of viewing file contents, for the most part you can use any of these three. There are some slight differences between them, so for the most part it comes down to personal preference. more and less split things by pages by default, where cat displays the whole file without stopping. Less allows you to move up through the file, rather than just down.

grep

Grep is commonly used to filter output. Sometimes there are multiple grep commands with the pipe character '|' between them.

grep PATTERN

returns lines in the output that include the word pattern (case sensitive)

grep -i PATTERN

returns lines in the output that include the word pattern (ignore case, could be uppercase or lowercase or mixed)

grep -v pattern

excludes lines with the word pattern from the result

grep -o pa.*rn

Includes only the items matched by the sample regular expression, rather than the entire line(s)

wc

wc prints counts. Although there are options for byte counts, character counts, word counts, and line counts the most common is line counts.

For line a lowercase L is used, so the syntax would be 'wc -l'

sort

Sort can be used to sort the output. In some cases we may want to sort by a specific column. A specific column can be specified with -k. Additionally, if you want to use a different delimiter you can use the '-t' option. The command "sort -k3 -n -t '|' " would sort by the third column, treat it as a number, and treat the pipe as the delimiter. '-r' reverses the sort order.

Let's take a look at a few examples. The first is just a partial directory listing. In the second example, we have added a sort by column 5 which is file size. From a basic sort perspective, 1 comes before 4, but the whole number is 12288 compared to 4095. In the third example, we use the additional modifier of '-n' to tell the sort to treat it as a number and look at the whole value, not just character by character left to right.

[root@fs82 forescout]# ls -al | grep _fsservice

drwxr-xr-x 37 _fsservice _fsservice   4096 Apr 6 13:18 .

drwxr-xr-x 2 _fsservice _fsservice 12288 Apr 6 09:28 backup

drwxr-xr-x 96 _fsservice _fsservice 20480 Apr 6 14:34 etc

drwxr-xr-x 6 _fsservice _fsservice   4096 Apr 6 08:58 modules

drwxr-xr-x 3 _fsservice _fsservice   4096 Apr 6 08:58 modules_ac

drwxr-xr-x 2 _fsservice _fsservice   4096 Apr 21 2021 policy

drwxr-xr-x 2 _fsservice _fsservice   4096 Apr 8 2019 reports

drwxr-xr-x 50 _fsservice _fsservice   4096 Apr 6 08:58 rollback

drwxr-xr-x 3 _fsservice _fsservice   4096 Apr 8 2019 spool

drwxr-xr-x 2 _fsservice _fsservice   4096 Apr 6 08:49 stats

drwxr-xr-x 2 _fsservice _fsservice   4096 May 1 2021 telemetry

drwxr-xr-x 2 _fsservice _fsservice   4096 Apr 6 08:58 tmp

drwxr-xr-x 3 _fsservice _fsservice   4096 Jan 26 11:38 upgrade

```
drwxr-xr-x 15 tomcat5    _fsservice    4096 Jan 26 11:48
webapps

[root@myem forescout]# ls -al | grep _fsservice | sort -k5

drwxr-xr-x  2 _fsservice _fsservice   12288 Apr  6 09:28 backup

drwxr-xr-x 96 _fsservice _fsservice   20480 Apr  6 14:34 etc

drwxr-xr-x  2 _fsservice _fsservice    4096 Apr 21  2021 policy

drwxr-xr-x  2 _fsservice _fsservice    4096 Apr  6 08:49 stats

drwxr-xr-x  6 _fsservice _fsservice    4096 Apr  6 08:58 modules

drwxr-xr-x  3 _fsservice _fsservice    4096 Apr  6 08:58
modules_ac

drwxr-xr-x 50 _fsservice _fsservice    4096 Apr  6 08:58 rollback

drwxr-xr-x  2 _fsservice _fsservice    4096 Apr  6 08:58 tmp

drwxr-xr-x 37 _fsservice _fsservice    4096 Apr  6 13:18 .

drwxr-xr-x  2 _fsservice _fsservice    4096 Apr  8  2019 reports

drwxr-xr-x  3 _fsservice _fsservice    4096 Apr  8  2019 spool

drwxr-xr-x  3 _fsservice _fsservice    4096 Jan 26 11:38
upgrade

drwxr-xr-x 15 tomcat5    _fsservice    4096 Jan 26 11:48
webapps

drwxr-xr-x  2 _fsservice _fsservice    4096 May  1  2021
telemetry

[root@myem forescout]# ls -al | grep _fsservice | sort -k5 -n

drwxr-xr-x 15 tomcat5    _fsservice    4096 Jan 26 11:48
webapps

drwxr-xr-x  2 _fsservice _fsservice    4096 Apr 21  2021 policy
```

```
drwxr-xr-x  2 _fsservice _fsservice  4096 Apr  6 08:49 stats

drwxr-xr-x  2 _fsservice _fsservice  4096 Apr  6 08:58 tmp

drwxr-xr-x  2 _fsservice _fsservice  4096 Apr  8  2019 reports

drwxr-xr-x  2 _fsservice _fsservice  4096 May  1  2021
telemetry

drwxr-xr-x 37 _fsservice _fsservice  4096 Apr  6 13:18 .

drwxr-xr-x  3 _fsservice _fsservice  4096 Apr  6 08:58
modules_ac

drwxr-xr-x  3 _fsservice _fsservice  4096 Apr  8  2019 spool

drwxr-xr-x  3 _fsservice _fsservice  4096 Jan 26 11:38
upgrade

drwxr-xr-x 50 _fsservice _fsservice  4096 Apr  6 08:58 rollback

drwxr-xr-x  6 _fsservice _fsservice  4096 Apr  6 08:58 modules

drwxr-xr-x  2 _fsservice _fsservice 12288 Apr  6 09:28 backup

drwxr-xr-x 96 _fsservice _fsservice 20480 Apr  6 14:34 etc
[root@myem forescout]#
```

Saving output to a file
The greater than symbol can be used to save output to a file.

'ls >/tmp/test.txt' would save the output from the command 'ls' to the file /tmp/test.txt

If the greater than symbol is used twice it would append output to a file.

'date >>/tmp/test.txt' would append the time to the existing file

Additionally, there are times that you may want to both export the information to a file as well as view it. For tee, '-a' is used to append.

'ls -al | tee -a /tmp/testfile.txt' will both list the directory and save the directory listing to a file.

timeout

The timeout command can be used to cancel a command after a certain period of time. If you have a command that you think may not finish in a specific time, you can use the timeout command.

$(command)

There are times that you may want to evaluate something and use the output in another command.

| tee /tmp/$(hostname)_test.txt

In this command example, the hostname would be used in the name of the output filename.

racadm

The racadm commands let you view the idrac configuration from an SSH session for a physical appliance or EM (not available on older hardware revisions). Additionally you can also set configuration from the command line without having to reboot the device to edit settings from the BIOS. If you set the IP address it will not reply immediately, it will take roughly 30 seconds to reinitialize and respond to the attempt to connect by HTTP or ping the address.

Some samples, the first one to retrieve information, the second one as an example for setting the IP address.

racadm getniccfg

racadm setniccfg -s 10.10.10.10 255.255.255.0 10.10.10.1

Root Access

Newer versions restrict the ability to log in via SSH as the root user. New installations of 8.2.2 or later have additional configuration if you wish to enable this. It can be enabled while logged in as cliadmin with the command 'ssh_root_password_login enable'. Otherwise, you will need to log in as cliadmin and then use the shell command in order to get to the root shell. When you enable this, the password for root will be the password that you have set with the command 'shell set-password'. This affects new installations of 8.2.2 or higher. Devices upgraded from previous versions may not be affected.

File structure overview
The root directory for most of the forescout specific files on the appliance and EM is /usr/local/forescout

From there we have subdirectories for various items, including plugin, log, as well as additional directories for backup and other items. Plugins have their own directories under the plugin directory. It is not common to have any reason to edit plugin files directly, and direct modification of any files should generally only be done under the explicit direction of Forescout support. Occasionally you may want to review the install.properties file or local.properties file for a plugin, but most of the time, the log locations for both the plugins and logs like today.log are typically where you will want to concentrate your troubleshooting investigation.

Today Log
The today log is another place to look at when troubleshooting. It is located at: /usr/local/forescout/stats/today.log

This file shows output of various queue values and other items on a recurring basis. For most items, values are written once a minute, as shown by the Linux epoch timestamps in the file.

The most common item to investigate with the today.log file is usually queues. For queues, we have the following entries: size, bytes, add, drop, and peak. If the queue ends up reaching the peak value, there will be drops. If the queue never reaches the peak, then items may be delayed in processing.

cat /usr/local/forescout/stats/today.log | grep DB | grep queue | grep delay

This command will display the lines of the today.log that include DB, queue, and delay, in order to monitor delay items specifically for the DB queues.

cat /usr/local/forescout/stats/today.log | grep DB | grep queue | grep delay | grep -v \ 0$

The grep at the end will exclude lines that end with a space and a 0. In a typical environment, there will likely not be delay, and most of the unnecessary lines will be excluded from the output, leaving the more relevant data.

Trace Log

The trace file lists out various logging levels for a large number of internal system items. Things such as messaging between appliances and EM, web portals, plugin API calls are just some of the items covered by this file. The file is located at /usr/local/forescout/etc/fstrace.properties .

There are two parts of the logging configuration, setting the logging level for a category and enabling/disabling the logging for the category.

The four logging levels are:

- 'Error'
- 'Warning'
- 'Normal'
- 'Detailed'

If the properties are commented out, the first character of the line will be '#' and that category is disabled.

Typically, when working with Forescout support, they may ask you to uncomment the line by editing and removing the octothorpe character '#' from the start of the line. Additionally, you may be asked to increase the logging level for a category from normal to detailed. The log files that get populated are Trace* log files, which are mainly in the /usr/local/forescout/log directory. When completed, make sure to put the logging categories back down to the initial levels. Turning on a several of these or setting to high values such as detailed can fill up drive space very quickly.

Additionally, another method of analysis of Trace files such as the Trace_cu files is to open a file in Excel. You can open the file and select the vertical pipe '|' as a delimiter. From there, you can use the sort function to look at messages from a specific trace source, or can sort by category.

Service Delay

Earlier we mentioned the importance to keep the 'big picture' in mind. Once you have refined a command to minimize output, you may want to run it across your environment in order to see if there are any issues on other devices.

fstool oneach -c "cat /usr/local/forescout/stats/today.log | grep service.delay | grep -v \ 0$| grep \ stats\ "

This one gives an example of querying the environment for service delay. In a large environment, this may still leave a lot of noise, so we will refine a bit further in the following lines.

fstool oneach -c "cat /usr/local/forescout/stats/today.log | grep service.delay | grep -v \ 0$| grep \ stats\ | wc -l" | grep -v Done

Excluding zero entries, count of how many minutes had a service delay according to the today.log file. When dealing with the oneach command, it can be common to use the "grep -v Done" at the end, as we generally don't care about the lines of the appliances stating how many seconds they took.

fstool oneach -c "cat /usr/local/forescout/stats/today.log | grep service.delay | grep -v \ [0-9]$ | grep -v \ stats\ |grep -v \ [1-9][0-9]$ | grep -v \ [1-9][0-9][0-9]$| wc -l"

Since service delay is in milliseconds, even values in tens or hundreds may not be significant. In this example, we are excluding ones with a one, two, or three digits, leaving only entries greater than 1000. Further the wc -l further simplifies by having each appliance just give a count of the results. The net result is the appliance returning an answer for how many minutes it had a service delay of 1000 or greater. Most appliances will typically still return zero, but ones that return higher values may need further investigation. Remember the today.log stats are on a per minute basis, so the number will be how many minutes there was a service delay above 1000 milliseconds.

Sidekick

Some of the plugins support the functionality of using a sidekick file to trigger additional information written to the temp directory. One example is the switch plugin. First, create the file with the touch command:

touch /usr/local/forescout/plugin/sw/sidekick.sw

This will trigger various files to be written to the /tmp directory, including things like switch information, MAC addresses learned, and more. If asked for this information as part of a support ticket, you will also likely be asked to upload the information after compressing it with tar to create a file archive:

tar -czvf /tmp/sw-sidekick.tgs 'find /tmp/sidekick/sw_*'

Policy processing analysis

The today.log can also be used to check relative policy processing, which can help indicate if a specific check or subrule is taking significantly more resources than others.

fgrep pol.resolve. /usr/local/forescout/stats/today.log | tss dist

This command will give an output with four columns, the first being the check, the second being the count, the third being percentage and the fourth being total. With the command run as shown above, they are sorted in ascending order, so only the last few entries will need to be checked. Below is partial output from the bottom of the list.

pol.resolve.4932454364353466064.periodical@cu	2455	1.0	84.8
pol.resolve.2515874325943985078.periodical@cu	2455	1.0	85.8
pol.resolve.-8153258345423457980.periodical@cu	2726	1.1	86.9
pol.resolve.-7308964523459876443.periodical@cu	2911	1.2	88.1
pol.resolve.-8997867333258743405.periodical@cu	2916	1.2	89.3
pol.resolve.6412237543453333469.periodical@cu	2966	1.2	90.5
pol.resolve.-4250986324569244460.periodical@cu	2967	1.2	91.7
pol.resolve.2482345320976434575.periodical@cu	2967	1.2	92.8
pol.resolve.3726897623434342206.periodical@cu	5421	2.2	95.0
pol.resolve.2718281828454590186.periodical@cu	12293	5.0	100.0

In this case, I would only check the last two entries, as the relative percentages for the last two are higher than the others above.

In general, if there was a significant problem with a particular processing entry, the later entries would be several times higher than the ones above.

In order to look up the large numerical value listed to see what rule or subrule it corresponds to, you can either paste it into the policy manager page (include the '-' if a negative value) or search for the number in the XML export of your policy set and see what condition it matches. From there, take a close look at that policy item and confirm that it is scoped properly and only matching the appropriate endpoints.

Other FSTOOL commands

A few other miscellaneous fstool commands.

fstool sysmap

When run on the EM, this gathers overall general stats across the environment with formats that can be viewed graphically. For example, if you have a device that has an excessive amount of hosts or assigned switches to manage, this command can be used to identify the imbalances. Additional items include swap values for various plugins, memory used, CPU utilization, channel traffic levels. Files that are output include log, csv, and html.

fstool bwstats

See stats about traffic flows to the appliance or EM. Default is to gather stats and display every 60 seconds. Default is to show top 50 flows. It utilizes bwtop, and running the command will also show you the parameters it uses

fstool rename_admin_user

The GUI user 'admin' has full access to the interface. From a security perspective, you may want to rename this user. This command enables you to do this. Due to the changes that this command makes, it needs to be run while the Forescout services are stopped. Stop the services, use this command to rename the admin user, and then start the services again.

fstool topavg

This command can be used to watch CPU level and average for a specific process.

fstool netconfig

This command can be used to adjust the network configuration, including IP address or gateway for a standalone EM or appliance. For an HA node, rerun 'fstool ha setup' to make these changes.

fstool oneach

This command when run on the EM, will run a command on each of the appliances and then return the output. This can be used to check the same item or run the same command on all appliances at once. One of the questions that we asked in the earlier chapter was "is the problem happening on multiple devices?"

Once we have something that identifies a problem, typically a log entry or other identifiable error, we can use the 'fstool oneach' command in order to run the command on all the devices in the environment, and evaluate the results.

'-c' option to run against multiple devices concurrently

'-R' will also run the command on the Recovery Enterprise Manager

'-f' will allow you to specify a file of specific appliances to run the command on (by name or IP, one per line)

fstool oneach -c -f /etc/mylist.txt "command here"

fstool oneach -c -R "command here" (includes Recovery Manager)

SCP is treated as a special case within the oneach syntax. The command 'fstool oneach "scp /tmp/testfile.txt" ' will copy that file from the EM to each appliance, at the same target destination, without needing to explicitly specify a destination.

While it is not always necessary to include the command in quotes, sometimes the commands may have certain characters that necessitate the usage of the quotes. For example, lets take a look at the following two commands:

fstool oneach cat /etc/hostname | grep test

fstool oneach "cat /etc/hostname | grep test"

In the first command above, the command run on the appliances is cat /etc/hostname and the grep is performed on the EM parsing the result. In the second command, the cat command and the grep are both done on the appliance, with the result passed back to the EM.

So, what do you do if the command that you actually want to run on the appliance includes a double quote as part of the command? Well you have two options. One option is that you can use a backslash preceding the double quote, and the other option is that you can use the fstool oneach command without the command, and then enter the command on the next line.

For example, if you want to run the following command:

sample "test" command

[root@myem ~]#fstool oneach "sample \"test\" command"

or

[root@myem ~]#fstool oneach

and then pressing enter/return and you will be prompted with:

Command:

where you can just type the command and don't have to worry about the backslashes.

This can also be useful in cases where you have other characters like backslashes in the command to be executed as well.

We will present a few other examples of this later in the chapter.

fstool metasend

Metasend allows you to send an email from the command line. Additionally, you have the option to attach a file, in addition to the typical options of a subject and email address.

fstool metasend -a /tmp/myfile.txt SUBJECT myemail@gmail.com

fstool db diskspace

This command can be used to check the database table size for some of the main tables. Typically the one that is most likely to see a large value would be source_log, but other tables may grow to large sizes as well. In a worst case scenario, if the tables grow too large too quickly, they can fill up the drive and possibly cause database corruption. In most cases, the purger which runs periodically will clear things up before the drive partition space is exhausted.

DB fix/rescue/reset

In the earlier chapter, we discussed the possibility of services not starting on an appliance. In some cases this can be the result of database issues. We have a few commands that can be used to attempt to clear things up. As mentioned in the earlier chapter, there may be times where you see the services not starting up completely, as shown by the output of 'watch fstool service status' and seeing the services get partway through the process and then crashing and trying again.

fstool db fix

fstool db rescue

fstool data_reset all

These three commands can clear up a number of issues, however some data may be lost. 'fstool db fix' is generally least intrusive, 'fstool db rescue' drops and replaces the database, and 'fstool data_reset all' clears all entries out of the database. Configuration of the appliance is still maintained with data_reset, however host information will need to be relearned. In most cases it's easiest to start with db fix or db rescue, and if the services still don't start, proceed with trying data_reset all.

fstool ipmi sel_list

This command allows you to view the system event log from the command log. This can then be saved off to a file. Later in this chapter, we will look at some additional examples.

fstool pretty

This command changes the output of a log file, to make it appear in a more user-friendly format.

In this example, we are looking at the user directory log file - ad.log

ad:64000:1618966880.170466:Tue Apr 20 21:01:20 2021: main::plugin_dev_cb:970: DOT1X_NTKEY2_READY [1]

ad:64000:1618966880.327984:Tue Apr 20 21:01:20 2021: started process:pid=64833,cmd=fstool ad_handle 10 1000

ad_handle:64833:1618966885.411763:Tue Apr 20 21:01:25 EDT -0400 2021: ad_handle main: msg = {config_md5=558bfdae0e12d76c

ed375f47c92f8931,type=learn_AD_groups,config={auth={dc01={ test_passwd=******,tlsv=none,test_user=marvin,filters=[sAMAcc o

untName,userPrincipalName],auth_method=,use_recursive_sea rch=,tlsparams={verifycrt=1,revocation=0,checkcrl=0,ocspsoft= 0,

clientcrt=0,ocsp=0},auth_dn_pattern=example.com,shrd_scrt=* *****}},dyn_dc={},console_login={dc01={test_passwd=******,tls

params={verifycrt=1,revocation=0,checkcrl=0,ocspsoft=0,client crt=0,ocsp=0},auth_dn_pattern=example.com,tlsv=none,test_u s

er=marvin,auth_method=,shrd_scrt=******}},idx={dc01=dc01},all ={dc01={base_dn=example.com,dyn_dc=0,dyn_refresh=3600,ip s_d

ata=[{ip_addr=172.16.159.199,accessed_by=}],type=ad,port=38
9}},dir={dc01={tlsv=none,test_user=marvin,filters=[sAMAccount

Name,userPrincipalName],ad_include_parent_groups=,_exists_
=1,ad_dynamic_primary_group=1,passwd=******,page_size=1000
,tls

params={verifycrt=1,revocation=0,checkcrl=0,ocspsoft=0,client
crt=0,ocsp=0},bind_user=marvin,ad_vendor=ad}}},this_node_id

Next, lets take a look at the same command using the 'pretty'
option:

cat ad.log | fstool pretty

ad:64000:1618966880.170466:Tue Apr 20 21:01:20 2021:
main::plugin_dev_cb:970: DOT1X_NTKEY2_READY [1]

ad:64000:1618966880.327984:Tue Apr 20 21:01:20 2021:
started process:pid=64833,

cmd=fstool ad_handle 10 1000

ad_handle:64833:1618966885.411763:Tue Apr 20 21:01:25 EDT
-0400 2021: ad_handle main: msg = {

    config_md5=558bfdae0e12d76ced375f47c92f8931,

    type=learn_AD_groups,

    config={

        auth={

            dc01={

```
                    test_passwd=******,

                    tlsv=none,

                    test_user=marvin,

filters=[sAMAccountName,userPrincipalName],

                    auth_method=,

                    use_recursive_search=,

                    tlsparams={

                            verifycrt=1,

                            revocation=0,

                            checkcrl=0,

                            ocspsoft=0,

                            clientcrt=0,

                            ocsp=0

                    },

                    auth_dn_pattern=example.com,

                    shrd_scrt=******

                }

        },

        dyn_dc={


        },

        console_login={

                dc01={
```

```
                test_passwd=******,

                tlsparams={

                        verifycrt=1,

                        revocation=0,

                        checkcrl=0,

                        ocspsoft=0,

                        clientcrt=0,

                        ocsp=0

                },

                auth_dn_pattern=example.com,

                tlsv=none,

                test_user=marvin,

                auth_method=,

                shrd_scrt=******

        }

},

idx={

        dc01=dc01

},

all={

        dc01={

                base_dn=example.com,

                dyn_dc=0,
```

267

```
                    dyn_refresh=3600,

                    ips_data=[{

                            ip_addr=172.16.159.199,

                            accessed_by=

                    }],

                    type=ad,

                    port=389

            }

        },

        dir={

            dc01={

                tlsv=none,

                test_user=marvin,

filters=[sAMAccountName,userPrincipalName],

                ad_include_parent_groups=,

                _exists_=1,

                ad_dynamic_primary_group=1,

                passwd=******,

                page_size=1000,

                tlsparams={

                        verifycrt=1,

                        revocation=0,

                        checkcrl=0,
```

```
                    ocspsoft=0,

                    clientcrt=0,

                    ocsp=0
            },
            bind_user=marvin,

            ad_vendor=ad
        }
     }
  },
  this_node_id=
```

--More--

Notice the formatting differences.

SQL introduction

While under most circumstances you will never need to run SQL commands on the appliance, there is the chance that you might be asked to run some as part of troubleshooting a support ticket. If you have run the commands listed above, such as fstool db diskspace or one of the other fstool db commands, you may be familiar with some of the table names. This is not intended to be an all inclusive tutorial, but rather coverage of some basic query examples.

In KB article 11108, they provide an example for taking all the entries from the np_action table and outputting to a text file. While the syntax shown may work just fine in a small scale environment, it could cause issues in a large deployment where the table has hundreds of thousands or millions of entries. In general, it is typically best to be granular in your queries rather than just asking for all the records.

Here we will look at a few examples. Note: tablename is not the name of an actual table in this database.

Select all records from a table (not recommended)

psql -c "select * from tablename"

Retrieve a total count of rows for a table

psql -c "select from tablename"

Notice that the only difference between these two is that that the one to retrieve all records has an asterisk '*', where the one that just retrieves the row count does not.

psql -c "select * from tablename LIMIT 10"

The LIMIT option will just receive a certain number of rows, 10 in this case. This can be useful if you just want to see the columns and some sample entries, before crafting a more granular query. Limiting to a small number of records uses significantly less CPU and memory resources than querying for ALL the rows.

you can add additional clauses, such as 'where' to further restrict the results

For numeric fields, such as time, you can use the greater than and less than symbols. For text values, use single quotes around the values. You can match a value exactly with the equals sign '=' .

psql -c "select from tablename where time>1649000000 "

This will select records with a value for the time field greater than a specified value.

If you have multiple clauses, you only use the word 'where' once, and then use 'and' for additional matches.

psql -c "select from devinfo where category='ad' and time>1649123456"

Earlier, we mentioned the commands fstool ip2int and fstool int2ip. In the database tables, dotted decimal format is not used, but rather a numeric value for the IP address. If you want to see what the corresponding value for an entry in a table, use the command fstool int2ip in order to convert the integer value to dotted decimal. Similarly, if you wanted to construct a query for a specific IP address, you could use the command 'fstool ip2int' at the command line. Optionally, you could use the command within the query itself.

psql -c "select from tablename where ip=$(fstool ip2int 10.10.10.10) "

Sometimes you want to match a blank field value. For the clear field, as an example, if the item has been cleared, the field gets set to 't' for true. Otherwise, the field is blank.

psql -c "select from np_action where clear is null"

Row count for uncleared actions for np_action table.

And here are a few additional examples, included as reference.

psql -c "select from tablename where time>$((-30 + $(date +%s))) "

Row count for a table for records with a time within the past 30 seconds.

psql -c "select action_id, count(action_id) from np_action where action_name='dot1x_authorize' and ip='18000000' and clear is null group by action_id | sort -k3 -n

Provide a count of various dot1x_authorize actions both manual and policy based for a specific address where the action is still active (hasn't been cleared), and then sort by column 3, treating it as numeric.

psql -c "select ip, count(ip) from np_action where action_name='dot1x_authorize' and clear is null group by ip" | sort -k3 -n

Provide a count of dot1x actions sorted by IP, to see if you have multiple uncleared actions for a single host.

Case Study - Failed Drive

Someone was walking through the datacenter and noticed that one of the hard drives on a Forescout appliance had a red indicator light like there was a hard drive issue. But they didn't remember which one it was. You could walk over to the datacenter and inspect the appliances individually, or could could use the information you've learned in this chapter to go beyond just this particular issue and inspect whether there are other drive failures in the environment, remembering the importance of the 'big picture'.

273

timeout 30 fstool oneach -c " fstool ipmi sel_list >/tmp/sel_list.txt "

This command will gather the system event log list on appliances and save to a temp file.

timeout 30 fstool oneach -c "ssha him fstool ipmi sel_list >/tmp/sel_list2.txt"

For appliances that are part of an HA pair, this will save the log list of the standby nodes to a temp file on the active node.

timeout 30 fstool oneach -c

      sed -i -e "s/^/$(hostname) /" /tmp/sel_list.txt

For the first file, this two line combo will prepend the active node's hostname to the temp file.

timeout 30 fstool oneach -c

      sed -i -e "s/^/$(ssha him hostname) /" /tmp/sel_list2.txt

For the temp file for the standby log list, prepend the hostname of the standby node.

timeout 30 fstool oneach -c "cat /tmp/sel_list*.txt" | grep -v sel_list | grep -v Done >/tmp/master_sel_list.txt

Take the two temp files and save them to a file on the EM.

sed -i -e 's/^/MYEM: /' /tmp/master_sel_list.txt

In the event of multiple EM in the environment, prepend the EM name to the lines in the file.

When completed you will have a master list.

cat /tmp/master_sel_list.txt | grep Drive

grep Drive /tmp/master_sel_list.txt

Either of these commands will show you the lines with Drive Faults

You could review the file locally on the appliance, or you could send the file to yourself via email or SCP.

Case Study - Export Data

In earlier sections we talked about exporting data. In this case study we are going to look at manipulating the Data with Excel. In this case, we are going to use a pivotable to sort the output by appliance. In some cases, looking at the distribution can tell you whether you are primarily having an issue with just a few appliances, or if any specific errors are evenly spread throughout the environment.

In this case, we are looking at a random data set. Typically, when doing this type of analysis, it would be hosts matching a specific subrule that you are investigating or troubleshooting.

Excel Pivotables

Open the file with Excel

In the text import wizard:

Select Delimited, click Next

Select Comma as delimiter, uncheck tab as a delimiter

Leave the column types as general, or change to Text if desired

Click Finish

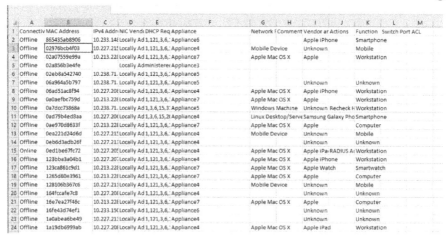

	A	B	C	D	E	F	G	H	I	J	K	L	M
1	Connectiv	MAC Address	IPv4 Addr	NIC Vend	DHCP Req	Appliance		Network I	Comment	Vendor ar	Actions	Function	Switch Port ACL
2	Offline	865435ab8906	10.233.14{	Locally Ad	1,121,3,6,:	Appliance6				Apple iPhone		Smartphone	
3	Offline	02976bcb4f03	10.227.21!	Locally Ad	1,121,3,6,:	Appliance4		Mobile Device		Unknown		Mobile	
4	Offline	02a07559e99a	10.213.22{	Locally Ad	1,121,3,6,:	Appliance7		Apple Mac OS X		Apple		Workstation	
5	Offline	02a856b3e4fe		Locally Administere	Appliance3								
6	Offline	02eb8a542740	10.238.71.	Locally Ad	1,121,3,6,:	Appliance5							
7	Offline	06a964a5b797	10.238.71.	Locally Ad	1,121,3,6,:	Appliance5				Unknown		Unknown	
8	Offline	06ad51ac8f94	10.227.20{	Locally Ad	1,121,3,6,:	Appliance4		Apple Mac OS X		Apple iPhone		Workstation	
9	Offline	0a0aefbc759d	10.213.22{	Locally Ad	1,121,3,6,:	Appliance7		Apple Mac OS X		Apple		Workstation	
10	Offline	0a7dcc73868a	10.238.71.	Locally Ad	1,3,6,15,3	Appliance5		Windows Machine		Unknown	Recheck H	Workstation	
11	Offline	0ad79b4ed8aa	10.227.20{	Locally Ad	1,3,6,15,2(	Appliance4		Linux Desktop/Serve		Samsung Galaxy Pho		Smartphone	
12	Offline	0ae970d8633f	10.213.22{	Locally Ad	1,121,3,6,:	Appliance7		Apple Mac OS X		Apple		Computer	
13	Offline	0ea221d24d6d	10.227.21!	Locally Ad	1,121,3,6,:	Appliance4		Mobile Device		Unknown		Mobile	
14	Offline	0eb6d3adb26f	10.227.21!	Locally Ad	1,121,3,6,:	Appliance4				Unknown		Unknown	
15	Online	0ed1be67fc72	10.227.20{	Locally Ad	1,121,3,6,:	Appliance4		Apple Mac OS X		Apple iPa	RADIUS A(	Workstation	
16	Offline	123bba3a04b1	10.227.20;	Locally Ad	1,121,3,6,:	Appliance4		Apple Mac OS X		Apple iPhone		Workstation	
17	Offline	123ca861c9d1	10.213.22{	Locally Ad	1,121,3,6,:	Appliance7		Apple Mac OS X		Apple Watch		Smartwatch	
18	Offline	1265d80e3961	10.213.22{	Locally Ad	1,121,3,6,:	Appliance7		Apple Mac OS X		Apple		Computer	
19	Offline	128106b367c6	10.227.21!	Locally Ad	1,121,3,6,:	Appliance4		Mobile Device		Unknown		Mobile	
20	Offline	164fccafe7c8	10.227.20{	Locally Ad	1,121,3,6,:	Appliance4				Unknown		Unknown	
21	Offline	16e7ea27f48c	10.213.22{	Locally Ad	1,121,3,6,:	Appliance7		Apple Mac OS X		Apple		Computer	
22	Offline	16fe43d74ef1	10.233.15{	Locally Ad	1,121,3,6,:	Appliance6				Unknown		Unknown	
23	Offline	1a0abea6be49	10.227.21!	Locally Ad	1,121,3,6,:	Appliance4				Unknown		Unknown	
24	Offline	1a19db6999ab	10.227.20{	Locally Ad	1,121,3,6,:	Appliance4		Apple Mac OS X		Apple iPad		Workstation	

Ctrl-A to select all

Select the Insert Tab and select Pivotable

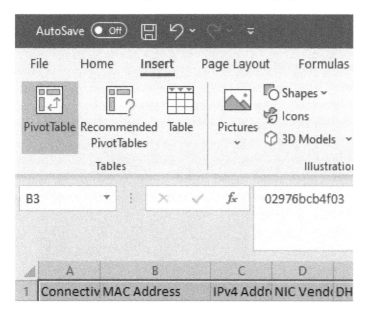

277

Since you selected the range, the table/range should be prepopulated

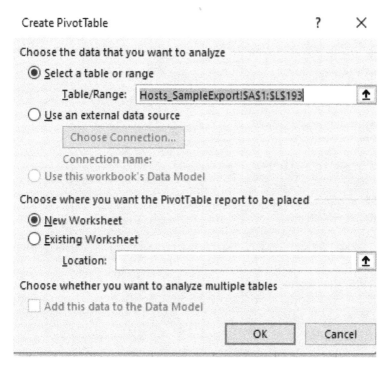

Choose placed in a new workbook, select OK.

On the PivotTable Fields, drag Appliance to the Rows box, and to the Sigma Values box

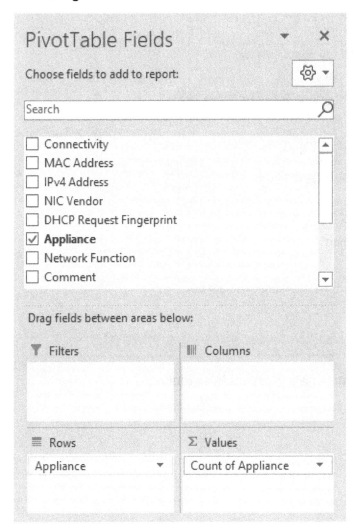

Almost there, we can see the data now.

	A	B
1		
2		
3	Row Labels ▾	Count of Appliance
4	appliance1	1
5	Appliance2	3
6	Appliance3	1
7	Appliance4	106
8	Appliance5	16
9	Appliance6	24
10	Appliance7	41
11	Grand Total	192
12		

Click the down arrow next to the column labels and select "More Sort Options"

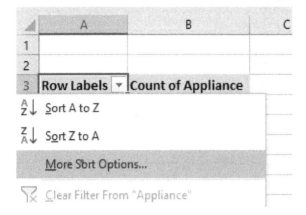

Select sort option of Descending, and in the drop down box select Count of Appliance.

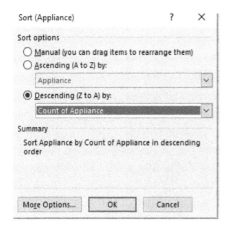

Now you can see which appliances have the most hosts for the selection by viewing the Pivotable.

Row Labels ↓	Count of Appliance
Appliance4	106
Appliance7	41
Appliance6	24
Appliance5	16
Appliance2	3
Appliance3	1
appliance1	1
Grand Total	192